/ff

ENDURING FREEDOM

An Afghan Anthology

FireStep Press

FireStep Publishing
Gemini House
136-140 Old Shoreham Road
Brighton
BN3 7BD

www.firesteppublishing.com

First published by FireStep Press, an imprint
of FireStep Publishing in 2011

A CIP catalogue reference for this book is available in the British Library.

ISBN 978-1-908487-01-8

Designed by FireStep Publishing
Cover by Ryan Gearing
Printed in the UK by Manor Creative – www.manorcreative.com

Printed on Munken Polar 300gsm (cover) 100 gsm (text)

ENDURING FREEDOM

An Afghan Anthology

Commemorating Operations in Afghanistan 2001-2011
Compiling Editor Ryan Gearing

FIRESTEP
Press

Dedication

To all those who served and who are still serving and their willingness to make the ultimate sacrifice defending freedom.

For James, for the future.

Contents

Foreword by His Grace, The Duke of Westminster   9

Acknowledgements   15

Introduction by Sir Andrew Motion   17

The Poems   19

Notes on Contributors / Authors   165

Foreword by His Grace, The Duke of Westminster

The debt we owe to our Armed Forces stretches back over the centuries and is forever increasing. Now we are asking our men and women to protect us by serving in Afghanistan. They are facing the most difficult of conditions and severe dangers and they are performing their tasks magnificently.

Some do, however, come home with scars either physical or mental. Combat Stress is a key charity for aiding those who cannot easily leave the tensions of the battlefield behind when they return to their families and I am delighted to be one of its supporters. In my years of service as a reservist I have met many people who needed the help of Combat Stress and many who are profoundly thankful that it exists to offer them support when it is needed,

Feeling as I do about Combat Stress I am delighted to support Ryan Gearing and Firestep Publishing in a most original initiative to publicise and raise more funds for this outstanding cause.

We all find different ways of coping with the demands of life. I have no doubt that poetry has been a great comfort to large numbers of our men and women as they faced danger in the combat zone. The work of Combat Stress must go on.

If

If you can keep your head when all about you
Are losing theirs and blaming it on you,
If you can trust yourself when all men doubt you,
But make allowance for their doubting too;
If you can wait and not be tired by waiting,
Or being lied about, don't deal in lies,
Or being hated, don't give way to hating,
And yet don't look too good, nor talk too wise:

If you can dream – and not make dreams your master;
If you can think – and not make thoughts your aim;
If you can meet with Triumph and Disaster
And treat those two impostors just the same;
If you can bear to hear the truth you've spoken
Twisted by knaves to make a trap for fools,
Or watch the things you gave your life to, broken,
And stoop and build 'em up with worn-out tools:

If you can make one heap of all your winnings
And risk it on one turn of pitch-and-toss,
And lose, and start again at your beginnings
And never breathe a word about your loss;
If you can force your heart and nerve and sinew
To serve your turn long after they are gone,
And so hold on when there is nothing in you
Except the Will which says to them: 'Hold on!'

If you can talk with crowds and keep your virtue,
Or walk with Kings – nor lose the common touch,
if neither foes nor loving friends can hurt you,
If all men count with you, but none too much;
If you can fill the unforgiving minute
With sixty seconds' worth of distance run,
Yours is the Earth and everything that's in it,
And – which is more – you'll be a Man, my son!

By Rudyard Kipling

Poem chosen by His Grace, The Duke of Westminster

Extract from Suicide In The Trenches

'You smug faced crowds with kindled eye
Who cheer when soldier lads march by
Sneak home and pray you'll never know
The hell where youth and laughter go'.

Siegfried Sassoon, 1917
Copyright Siegfried Sassoon by kind permission of the Estate of George Sassoon

Extract from Here Dead We Lie

'Life, to be sure, is nothing much to lose,
But young men think it is,
And we were young.'

AE Housman, 1919

The picture opposite is of my son, a serving Sergeant with 2 PWRR, at Roshan Tower, Afghanistan, two years ago. The picture was taken by C/Sgt 'Dutch' Holland of 2 PWRR just as the first incoming RPG landed in the compound on the last day of the siege.

The picture says it all really and I always accompany it with the poem extracts above.

Photograph and poem extracts submitted by Alain Chissel

Acknowledgements

I owe some particular thanks to those who have helped in the support and preparation of my first personal foray into publishing. Usually I rely on others doing the writing or submissions so working both sides of the fence at the same time has been an interesting challenge – in no particular order; Geoff Simpson, Bridget Kennington, Sir Andrew Motion, His Grace, The Duke of Westminster, Sarah Fellows, Lieutenant Colonel 'JB' Brown, Michael Brett, Katy Marshall, Colonel TJ Hodgetts, Jeanette Gavin, Graham Hales, Lisa Youd, Carolyn Jones, Phil Welsh, Steven Atkinson, ARRSE, Martin Mace, Helen Tovey, Vicky Thomas; Hal Stewart, Mike Howarth and everyone at BFBS, Neil Cox, Nicola Hudson, Jo Grace, Janice Lobban and the rest of the Combat Stress team and anyone else, I am sorry if I have neglected you by name – you know who you are. Special thanks are due to Arctic Paper for their generous support of this anthology.

Thank you to all those who contributed to this anthology, we all share the same respect for the men and women who serve in HM Forces, and to those personnel, serving and veterans, thank you for allowing our continued freedoms.

I would also like to thank Steve Bucknell, Johnathan Bourne, Anne Bevis, Ted Sharpe, Chris Wannell and Jim Whelan at Wootton Bassett for having the belief and their support not only in this work but who have showed the world an amazing empathy and honour towards those in our military. Thank you for allowing this book to be launched on such hallowed ground.

Finally I would like to thank my wife, Sarah who really is the most understanding and is always there to support my publishing endeavours. Thank you.

Introduction by Sir Andrew Motion
Poet Laureate 1999-2009

Most people, when asked what they think a 'war poem' might be, are likely to give
an answer that includes a mention of Wilfred Owen. And they'd be right to do so.
Owen, like Sassoon, Rosenberg, Graves, Gurney and Blunden, give an account
in their poems of 'the war to end all wars' that did not end them at all – but
nevertheless set an unforgettable pattern for what war poetry in general might
be and contain. Face to face fighting. Trenches. Mud. Slaughter on an epic scale.
Heroic suffering and endurance.

There's plenty to be said in favour of this pre-eminence. The best poems of the
First World War are very good, and they guarantee that its catastrophe will never
be forgotten. But at the same time, the fame of Owen et al inhibits the reputation
of later war poets, who inevitably describe the different circumstances of later
conflicts in different ways. Where Owen in 'Strange Meeting' describes fighting his
enemy hand to hand ('I parried, but my hands were loath and cold'), the greatest
poet of the Second World War, Keith Douglas, describes a clinical and problematic
detachment ('Now in my dial of glass appears/the soldier who is going to die').
Readers have been reluctant to accept these differences of circumstance and tone
between the two 'world wars' – just as they have also been slow to accept the
different kinds of war poetry produced during the war in Vietnam and in other, later
theatres of conflict. It can hardly be called Owen's fault, but the fact is: his poems
have created a kind of shadow, in which other sorts of war poetry than his have
found it difficult to find the readership they deserve.

This anthology is, among other things, a brave and valuable attempt to break
this stranglehold. Which is partly to say; its great strength lies in its variety. Some
of the poems it contains are by dead professionals (Kipling and Housman, for
instance). Some are by people who evidently have a distinct formal training and
expertise. But the great majority are by men and women who write not because they
are in some sense trained to do so, but because they recognise that poetry has a
primitive authority in the wider world they want to address.

'Enduring Freedom', in other words, is invigorating mixture of polished and
homespun, deliberated and impulsive, outspoken and whispered, dogmatic and
slant, cooked and raw. This is its greatest strength as a collection of pieces of
writing. Looked at from another point of view, a human point of view, it is a startling
record of courage, stoicism, dedication and affection. For all these reasons, it
deserves a wide and admiring readership.

The Poems

SALLY AINSWORTH
A Marine Mum's Smile   25
'Our Promise'   26
The Knock And Car Doors Shutting At Night   27

MARK ANDREWS
Royal Navy Suez Canal Transit   28

ANON
Weapons   29
A Very Special Christmas Message   30

MIKE BEAVIS
30 Minutes   33
My Girl Is Waiting   35
Parade!   37
RIP Royal   38
The Unsung   39

LAURENCE BINYON
For The Fallen   40

BLACKDOG661
Black Dog   42
My Wife Went To London   43
The Great Leveller   45
Who Are THEY?   46
Why Do I Call It 'Black Dog'?   48

NEIL BLOWER
Buffy   50
Last Post   51
The Poppy   52
That Face   53
The Brightest Light   54
The Poet   55
Why We Fight   56
Wootton Bassett   57

JULIA BOND
An Army Wife   58
My Little Girl   59

PETER BRANSON
Into The Jaws Of Death   60
Mummy's Boy   61

MICHAEL BRETT
Bomb Attack   62
Bomb Circuitry   63
The Entry Of Osama Bin Laden Into Paradise   64
Feeding The War Gods In This Age Of Miracles   65
Machine Gun   66
Mosques And Rockets   67
Suicide Bomber   68
9/11 Poem From London: Tomorrow It Will All Run Backwards   69

CHARLIE BROWN
They Gave Me A Medal   70

JB BROWN
A Reckoning   71
Do Not Hesitate   72
God Allows An Angel To Die   73
Judgement Has Found You Worthy   74
Of The Oleander   75
Stealing Stars   76
The Availability Of The Dead   77
The Baghdad Cigar Aficionado Club   78
The Battle List & The Way Ahead   79
The Boneyard   80
The Conservation Of Angular Momentum   81
The Great Debate   82
The Promise Of Things To Come   84
Where Your Ashes Kiss The Earth   85

KATIE BUTLER-MANUEL
War   86

DANIEL CLAYTON
Tour Of Duty   87

MARTIN CROWSON
A Soldier's Battle Thought   89

JO De VRIES
Valentine From Kabul   90

GEORGE DOUGLAS
A Mother's Soldier Comes Home 91

STEVEN FIRKINS
Art Of War 92
Brotherhood 93
Cross The Line 94
Distant Peace 95
Queen And Country 96
The End 97
The Night 98
Welcome To The Valley 99

CLEVELAND W. GIBSON
Dear Husband 100
Old Soldier 101

IVOR GURNEY
Strange Hells 102

STEVE HALLIWELL
What Makes A Hero's Road 103

JODIE HENDERSON
Lone Chimes 104

STEVEN LESLIE HILL
Foot Patrol 105

TJ HODGETTS
Dressing The Dead 107
Sangin Valley 108
Solifugit 110
Death Of A Clock 111
Amputee 112
A Hymn For Helmand 114

DEAN HORTON
The Airborne Medic's Creed 115

IAN JOLLEY & MICHAEL MALIN
Wife, Friend, Lover 116

HENRY KEMPSTER
The Casualty 118

RUDYARD KIPLING
The Young British Soldier   119

JG MAGEE
High Flight   121

PAUL MARLOW
Orphan   122
Rant   123
Rapid Eye Movement   124
Split-Frame   125

NIGEL MARSHALL
Sleeping Out At Christmas   126

PAIGE McALWANE
Against The War   128
Oh Dear Sweet Child Of Mine   130

MICHAEL McKENZIE
Soul Mates   131

JAMES MILTON
A New Jerusalem   133
A Soldier's Lot   135
A Soldier's Prayer   137
Child's Play   138
Death Or Dishonour   139
Coming Home   140
The Wife's Prayer   141

NEALE MOSS
A Time For Reflection   142

LIAM O'BRIEN
The War In My Head   144

PHOENIX
The Reality Of The Unreality   145

THOMAS ROBERTS
Bulletin   147

MICHAEL RODGERSON
Weep For The Soldier   148

STEVE SELL
Cry For Me Not   149
This Is My Field Now   150

KEVIN SMYTHERS
They Serve - For Our Freedom...   151

JANE STEMP
Waiting For The Truce   153

BARBARA STOCKER
Day Of Remembrance   154

MARK THURLEY
The Journey   155

SHEILA WEBB
The Humble Poppy   156
Two Minutes' Silence - We Must Remember Them   157
Stand And Be Counted   158
Wootton Bassett - A Salute   159
War Memorial   160

SONJA WHALEN
A Sad Silent Miracle   161
My Dear Lost Picture   162

ROSA WILLIAMS
Friend's Soliloquy 1943   163

SALLY AINSWORTH

A Marine Mum's Smile

Just look a little behind the smile
of a Royal marine's mum

She smiles with pride
but the lines show her worry

Her eyes they smile
But her mind's far away

She tells herself to stop
He will be okay

She lives in the moment
but no-one knows her fear

She needs a cuddle or that smile will fade
She needs the cuddle from her Marine her Son
then she know's he is ok

'Our Promise'

I watched, as you walked away
You told me to be brave

You said to let you go
In the usual way

Did you know how hard it was?
To smile when my heart was breaking
But I did what you asked of me

Now all I ask of you
Is to keep your promise

'That you will come home to me'

The Knock And Car Doors Shutting At Night

On my door is a notice
Do not knock
Knock on the window

I fear the knock as do thousands of military mums
Please do not knock

At night I hear the car doors shut
Please please do not knock on my door

I get out of bed to see
I do not want that knock

Are they coming to our door
Please do not knock

The only knock I want on my door
Is a surprise that my boy has come home safe early as a surprise
He can knock loudly
He is home safe

MARK ANDREWS

Royal Navy Suez Canal Transit

The hazy shimmering sands on either side of us,
remind me of two hot slices of golden-brown toast,
the Suez Canal in the middle, reminiscent of melting butter,
and the Ship, a breadcrumb, floating slowly towards the Red Sea.

If the Ship is a crumb then what are we sailors – tiny specks,
living, working and existing on the crumb under the relentless sun,
sweating more each passing day – in rivers down our red-brown bodies,
melting more each passing day – with love and longing for those left at home.

April 2002.

ANON

Weapons

There are many types of weapons
But the ones that hurt the most
Are the weapons made of memories
And the deadly midnight ghost
Not all wounds are red and bloody
...There are wounds that touch the mind
These are wounds that always fester
They're the never healing kind
Why are we who've done our duty
Plagued by wounds that never heal
Made by weapons of our memories
Which are worse than lead and steel

A Very Special Christmas Message

T'was the night before Christmas,
He lived all alone,
In a one-bedroom house,
Made of plaster and stone.

I had come down the chimney,
With presents to give,
And to see just who,
In this home, did live...

I looked all about,
A strange sight I did see,
No tinsel, no presents,
Not even a tree.

No stocking by mantle,
Just boots filled with sand,
On the wall hung pictures,
Of far distant lands

With medals and badges,
Awards of all kinds,
A sober thought,
Came through my mind.

For this house was different,
It was dark and dreary,
I found the home of a soldier,
Once I could see clearly.

The soldier lay sleeping,
Silent, alone,
Curled up on the floor,
In this one-bedroom home.

The face was so gentle,
The room in disorder,
Not how I pictured,
A true British soldier.

Was this the hero,
Of whom I'd just read?
Curled up on a poncho,
The floor for a bed?

I realised the families,
That I saw this night,
Owed their lives to these soldiers,
Who were willing to fight.

Soon round the world,
The children would play,
And grown-ups would celebrate,
A bright Christmas Day.

They all enjoyed freedom,
Each month of the year,
Because of the soldiers,
Like the one lying here..

I couldn't help wonder,
How many lay alone,
On a cold Christmas Eve,
In a land far from home.

The very thought brought,
A tear to my eye,
I dropped to my knees,
And started to cry.

The soldier awakened,
And I heard a rough voice,
'Santa don't cry,
This life is my choice;

I fight for freedom,
I don't ask for more,
My life is my god,
My country, my corps..'

The soldier rolled over,
And drifted to sleep,
I couldn't control it,
I continued to weep.

I kept watch for hours,
So silent and still,
And we both shivered,
From the cold night's chill.

I did not want to leave,
On that cold, dark, night,
This guardian of honour,
So willing to fight.

Then the soldier rolled over,
With a voice soft and pure,
Whispered, 'carry on Santa,
It's Christmas Day, all is secure.'

One look at my watch,
And I knew he was right.
'Merry Christmas my friend and to all a good night.'

This poem was written by a peacekeeping soldier stationed overseas.

MIKE BEAVIS

30 Minutes

30 minutes left at home and faster my heart starts to beat.
And so its time to go away again and yet I can't move my feet
I step out onto the landing and I hear a familiar sound,
She is starting the engine, its so unbelievably loud!
I haul my bergan onto my back,
I hear her call,
I push my way down the stairs, trying not to mark the walls.
She stands there at the bottom, she always manages a smile.
I kiss her on the forehead.
'It will only be for a little while'
We are in the car now, the seats full of camouflage bags,
We bump and squeak along as the suspension sags.
We look at each other and yet neither of us speaks.
My leave is over again,
too fast was my week.
And as we approach the station I glance at its clock,
The thought of leaving again I now try to block.
Who speeded up time?
Where has my leave gone?
At home or away,
I know not where I belong.
Seems like yesterday when I was pulling into the station,
When my love waited for me with sweet anticipation.
She watched soldiers arrive home, laughing like young lads,
hiding their secret burdens, behind massive issue bags.

Platform One for London Kings Cross.
I look into her eyes, and she looks so lost.
I hold her close and we share a long kiss,
As the train pulls in with a menacing hiss!
I start to pull away, she again pulls me near,
Breaking her heart is now all I fear.
'Give me a ring when you get to where you are going'
She smiles again now, with only her brave face showing.
'Will do' I say ' as soon as I get there.'
As I kiss her deeply and run my hands through her soft golden hair.
We struggle as always, but its time that pulls us apart.

Separated now
Emptiness filling our hearts.
Running to the train I risk that last look over my shoulder.
Longing to steal time, just longer to hold her.

I get inside and dumping my grip, loosening the straps,
off my shoulders it slips.
Always no seats so it's to the corridor for soldier class.
The train starts to move and time is stolen so fast.

My Girl Is Waiting

And so finally we're pulling in to the station.
My heart is pounding
My girl is waiting

Six months ago I left her standing where she stands now,
Trying to find strength,
To let go somehow

And with tears in her eyes and a voice of despair,
Another broken heart, now beyond repair.

How she has waited for me I will never know,
Just keeping it inside
Letting only courage show

And now all that separates us is the carriage I'm in,
The noise of returning soldiers, a comforting din.

And with a hiss, the train doors finally do part,
We make eye contact
A skipped beat in my heart,

As I reach for her, and she says my name,
Six months of pain are washed away, like a gentle summers rain.

I hold her now and time stands still
An empty vessel, my heart
Only she can fill.

And with a hiss of engines the train gets underway, moving down the track the
carriages sway

As I looked back I see another soldier
He smiles with his wife, so close he now holds her.

And in the back of my mind I know the day will come,
When I have to return to the sand and the scorching sun,
For this is the course we have chosen to run
But now with this war, my duty is done.

Duty now lies only with her,
My love, my protection
And back in my care

I can never tell her of the horrors I have seen,
She could never comprehend
How I have longed for her, so broken.
Wounds only she can mend

She doesn't ask questions,
No truth she seeks
Her hand through my hair and a kiss on my cheek

And tonight in each others' arms we lay,
I thank God I can hold her
We are together again...

Parade!

And we are all brought to attention with the next word of command.
We all gather to remember the dead,
Our brothers in the sand.
A small child cries for her daddy as they play the last post
The wind blows through us
A familiar icy ghost.
Stood like statues, we remember the lost
We questions if we have it in us?
Could we pay the ultimate cost?
They shall grow not old as we that are left grow old
But who will hold the young widows through the winters so cold?
Age shall not weary them nor the years condemn.
Is this a worthy conflict to sacrifice our country's men?
And at the going down of the sun, and in the morning we shall remember our boys.

While politicians continue to treat our soldiers like toys.
The Chaplain says his prayers, we join in with Amen.
We line the memorial with poppy wreaths ,
That icy wind cuts through us again.
The names of the fallen are read out in sombre monotone,
Those who fell in foreign fields,
The ones who never made it home.
We are then dismissed and marched off the square
We catch a glimpse of a sobbing woman
A veil of tears concealed by windswept hair.
And so it is to the unit bar with hearts heavy like lead.
And its with raised glasses, we remember.
Our glorious dead.

RIP Royal

Deep in sand, lands of war and toil,
Fighting for the free world is where you will find Royal.
His life for his mates, never one to be jack,
the weight of the world, he carries on his back.
So when one of the lads doesn't make it home,
and Op Minimise has shut down the phones,
we will say to the families 'You are never alone!'

Per Mare Per Terram, by sea by land.
To the loved ones we will hold out our hands.
The Royal Marines is the biggest family you will ever have!
And we pray to the big man to look after our lads!

The Unsung

They stand up, they are counted.
They stand where others dare not.
To them money is no motive, to fight in countries barren and hot.

They question not their duties,
For their country they fight.
Getting old beyond their years in lands of death and strife.

This is the burden that lies with the youth of today.
Fighting for a country that doesn't care,
That it is with their lives they pay.

How can we thank our men for giving up their youth?
For they are our heroes.
They have nothing left to prove.

They lay in dusty shell scrapes,
We sleep safe in our beds,
As the rounds keep coming in and mortars whistle over their heads!

And if they make it home we give them nothing but shit!
Asking stupid questions like 'did you get a confirmed hit?'

What type of question is that?
And what is it to you?
These men have seen violence,
And lost a friend or two!

So next time on Remembrance Day
When our heroes are out on parade
Take time to think of the sacrifices that they made!
And how many young lives were lost to keep what we love free.
And just what will the final death toll be?

Will it take that flag-draped coffin to contain your friend or your son?
Before you to ask why do our heroes remain unsung?

LAURENCE BINYON

For The Fallen

With proud thanksgiving, a mother for her children,
England mourns for her dead across the sea.
Flesh of her flesh they were, spirit of spirit,
Fallen in the cause of the free.

Solemn the drums thrill: Death august and royal
Sings sorrow up into immortal spheres.
There is music in the midst of desolation
And a glory that shines upon our tears.

They went with songs to the battle, they were young,
Straight of limb, true of eye, steady and aglow.
They were staunch to the end against odds uncounted,
They fell with their faces to the foe.

They shall grow not old, as we that are left grow old;
Age shall not weary them, nor the years condemn.
At the going down of the sun and in the morning
We will remember them.

They mingle not with laughing comrades again;
They sit no more at familiar tables of home;
They have no lot in our labour of the day-time;
They sleep beyond England's foam.

But where our desires are and our hopes profound,
Felt as a well-spring that is hidden from sight,
To the innermost heart of their own land they are known
As the stars are known to the night;

As the stars that shall be bright when we are dust,
Moving in marches upon the heavenly plain,
As the stars that are starry in the time of our darkness,
To the end, to the end, they remain.

By permission of The Society of Authors, literary representatives of the estate of Laurence Binyon.

Poem chosen by Ryan Gearing in memoriam to all those who have fought and served for our country. This poem has personal importance after having the privilege to deliver the exhortation; the fourth verse from the poem, at the Last Post Ceremony at the Menin Gate in Ypres (Ieper), Belgium.

BLACKDOG661

Black Dog

I can feel you watching me Black Dog
Waiting
Waiting
Waiting for the moment
Your patience inexhaustible

Sometimes Black Dog growls
or sniffs
or barks
Black Dog, why can't I train you?

When will you learn to obey,
like real dogs
or must I obey you?

Black Dog, am I your master
or you mine?
Why can't we co-exist, Black dog?
Black Dog, why do you sit and wait?
Black Dog, why don't you answer me?

My Wife Went To London

My wife went to London
to be interviewed
by the BBC
no less
about the struggle
and the strife
of being married
to a husband
with PTSD,
while remaining
a loving wife
(I might add)
whose love overbears
the strife.

When my wife went to London
she met the wife of a friend
and they both
have in common
the struggle and
the strife
of loving husbands
with PTSD.

When my wife went to London
she was interviewed
as was my friend's wife
and they found
much in common,
but
they also found a friend
in each other
who understood THEIR
daily struggle
against PTSD.

When my wife went to London
the interview to make
it was expected
to be heard
by thousands
most of whom
will know little
about the trouble
and the strife,
BUT some of whom
are struggling
to support their partners
in their struggle
with PTSD
and those with whom
our wives' words
have struck a chord
should know that
they too are not alone
they too have friends
who understand
their trouble and strife
with PTSD
They just have not
met them......Yet.

I would like to dedicate this poem to ALL partners and the health professionals who support them, in their struggle to help a loved one in their fight with PTSD.

The Great Leveller

'How tall are you?'
the Sergeant asked
'six foot one' I replied
'Bollocks' he retorted.
To the next in line,
the same question,
the reply to which
he only snorted.
To all in line,
the question asked
the replies to which,
he said were 'Arse'.
'You are only as tall'
the Khaki god intoned
'As your rifle –
      Forty three inches[1]'
As I was to learn
a rifle is called a weapon,
so pity today's soldier,
when the Battlefield on,
whose weapon is a mere
thirty one inches[2],
all told
and the poor Civvy[3],
who, despite making bold,
on his 'weapon'
has no inches at all!

[1] 43 Inches – the length of the SLR (Self Loading Rifle) – the standard British Army
rifle at the time (1980).
[2] 31 Inches – the length of the SA80 Assault Rifle (more correctly the Rifle 5.56 – the
current standard British Army Rifle.
[3] Civvy – Civilian.

Who Are THEY?

Who are THEY?
THEY live among *us*
and THEY say
THEY are apart of *us*
while THEY live apart
from *us*.
I think
THEY look down on *us*
and THEY secretly
hold *us* in contempt
Yet THEY seek our approval
Regularly
THEY say THEY work for **us**
But do THEY really?
NO!!
THEY do what
the big corporations
whisper in their ears
and tell them what
to do
When THEY are not
Kissing children
In front of adoring crowds
in a 'Photo op'

THEY are secretly working out
how THEY can steal
the children's sweets
THEY expect **us** to work longer
for less,
While taking more for themselves
Who are these freeloaders
Par excellence?
There is, for me
no longer
ANY difference between
Right
or Left
or Centre
THEY have sold **us ALL** into
economic slavery
(which is still slavery,
only the chains are different)
THEY are
Politicians.

Why Do I Call It 'Black Dog'?

Why Black Dog?
Someone once asked
It helps to give
your PTSD a form
I once was told.

So when I am down,
My mood is black,
Because
there is no hope,
no light
and no way back.

It is a dog
a Labrador
as a matter of fact,
and like a Labrador
it is always at my side
ever faithful
watching, waiting,
matching me
stride for stride.

Black Dog it is
for me,
a he and not a she,
for a female
means comfort and care
not something
that drives me spare,
and sends me
headlong
into oblivion.

And also
Churchill who suffered
Way before I
called his depression
the same.
If it's good enough for him
it is more than good enough
for I
That is why
it is
Black Dog.

NEIL BLOWER

Buffy

You were the first, of the many to come,
I'll love you forever, you helped me get some.
You will always have a special place in my heart,
and I'll never forget how I tore you apart.
You were my friend, my saviour, my light,
Before I went to sleep, I always held you tight.
The first time we did it, I was nervous as hell,
I sent one down your chamber and I wanted to yell.
I couldn't believe that I'd finally done it,
You made it so easy, it felt like I'd won it.
The ones that came after were just like the rest,
And I'll always remember that you were the best.
Thank you.

Buffy is about Neil's first rifle. In basic training you are encouraged to give your rifle a girl's name.

Last Post

The music starts and my eyes fill with tears. Will it be like this forever?
For all my remaining years.

The bugler blows and the flag is slowly lowered.
I can't hear that music and not think I'm a coward. Why am I here and they're
rotting in the ground?

The screams of young boys dying, lay writhing on the ground.
Then the music stops,

And the padre starts to speak. And I can't help but feel,
the redness of my cheeks.

The Poppy

From the blood of the trenches, something special grew.
A symbol of the old,
embraced by the new.

Whenever it's worn,
we all stop and stare.
A rallying cry for all those who care.

They say the guns fell silent a long time ago. But from Basra to Bastion,
we know this isn't so.

Ninety years on it's as needed as ever, but we can all only hope,
that it won't be forever.

What it's become is a legend to all,
and a symbol of hope to help us stand tall.

Whenever it's needed, it will always be there, to help those in need,
and show them we care.

That Face

That Face.
That Face in the darkness, as pure as the snow
That Face in the darkness where evil things grow
That Face.
Are you a monster or are you a man?
Innocence lost forever, but I'll do what I can.
That Face.
You stole something precious, a legend to all,
But my friend Jim made sure you'd fall.
That Face.
That Face in the void, the dark recesses of my mind,
I hope that you're glad,
That we repaid you in kind.
That Face.

The Brightest Light

I am the brightest light,
I am the darkest shadow,
I am the balance of justice,
I am the deep well of despair.

I am the darkness, I am the light,
I am the spirit that makes you willing to fight,
I am the shadows haunting your nights,
I am the strength that makes evil take flight.

I am the truth, I am the lie,
I am the child that wants you to fly,
I am life, I am death,
I am there when you take your first and last breath.

In the darkest night,
on the brightest day,
Always remember, never forget,
The darkest shadow,
Comes from the brightest day.

The Poet

Someone's goin' the emergency room
Someone's goin' to jail.
Is how the line goes.
Another sip of bourbon
and then the art flows.

Alone in the darkness
Alone with the thoughts
In a New York minute
Is what the voice taught.

Another dose of death
Then he takes another sip
The voice mentions love
Then he shoots from the hip.

Stories of loss, of love
of pain and despair,
of things that make life
worth living,
Then he never stops giving.

The crescendo's over.
The voice is long gone.
But in those three minutes,
Something special was done.

Why We Fight

Why do we fight?
My friend said to me,
'To kill the enemy of course, it fills us with glee'

That's what the conchies think, but let me tell you the truth, this ain't no anthem,
for a lot of doomed youth.

Across the whole Armed Forces,
the same story is told.
Civvys think we're heroes,
and that we're brave and we are bold.

Fight for Queen and country that's true
to a degree

But what we really fight for, is our family and yours

We fight for love and for friendship on tanks and great big ships,
all the while thinking,
of kissing our loved ones on the lips.

Wootton Bassett

Thank you, thank you,
from the bottom of my heart, the town of Wootton Bassett, for playing your big part.

You might not think it special, but I assure you that it's true, the whole United Kingdom owes a debt to you.

You taught us how to show respect, with dignity and with kind.
You put the grieving families,
at the forefront of our minds.

You're Royal now,
and about time too.
Thank you Wootton Bassett, you're a hero too.

JULIA BOND

An Army Wife

I wear no uniform, no blues or whites.
But I am in the Army because I am his wife.
I'm in the ranks that are rarely seen
I have no rank upon my shoulder.
Salutes I do not give.
But the military world is where I live.
I'm not the chain of command, orders I do not get.
But my husband is the one who does, this I cannot forget.
I'm not the one who fires the weapon, who puts my life on the line.
But my job is just as tough, I'm the one left behind.
My husband is a patriot, a brave and prideful man.
And the call to serve his country not all can understand.
Behind the lines I see the things needed to keep this country free.
My husband makes the sacrifice, but so do our kids and me.
I love the man I married, soldiering is his life,
But I stand among the silent ranks known as the Army Wife.

This poem was written by a friend of mine whilst we were in Guttersloh, 2007.

My Little Girl

The Army has taken my daddy away,
he's gone to the Falklands, so they say.
I don't think my daddy wanted to fight,
but it sometimes takes courage to do what is right.

We went to Portsmouth to wave him goodbye,
some people cheered, but I saw my mummy cry.
'God bless them all,' said a man in the crowd,
I thought of my dad and felt very proud.

The house seems so quiet since dad went away,
Mum listens for news on TV all day,
I hope he is safe and the seas aren't too rough,
I'm sure I'd be scared, but I know my dad's tough.

This poem was sent to me by my dad while he was serving in the Falklands conflict with 29 Commando Regiment, Royal Artillery, from HMS Intrepid, *June 14 1982.*

PETER BRANSON

Into The Jaws Of Death
'Some One Had Blunder'd'

(Tennyson: 'The Charge Of The Light Brigade')

Parade of faces, broadsheet wise, all spent:
Gibraltar Forward Operations Base,
Afghanistan, 2 Para, last week's news.

As liable to be killed or maimed as in
the First World War, you chase the Taliban
through corn high as an elephant's eye, point-blank:
pure comic book, like rabbits in headlights.

It's called 'The Mouth of Hell': the constant threat
of skirmish, mortar, sniper, mine, vest bomb;
phone pictures for the blokes back home – 'Respect!'

No wonders why or truck with politics,
the recipe: take youthful fervour, add
close comradeship, fall pride ('No holding back'),
incessant drill, adrenalin; stir well.

No pause for air cover, boots melting in
the sun, hit them head on: 'They choose the ground.
No sweat, we charge straight through their ambushes.'

June 12th, you're tossing sweets to kids who laugh
and point beyond the track across a stream.
You take a look. They open up, sheer weight
of fire indelible: 'Hard rock 'n' roll.'

'Man down!' You're hot as blazes till that first
shot's fired, then cold as ice: slow – quick, quick – slow,
weird time. Word's out two more have done and died

Mummy's Boy

These days, the widow's mite, a perfect son:
no dirty clothing, tissues, mugs and plates
laid down to clutter up his room, lad mags;
no bother at the school – 'out of control!',
or with the Police, 'Glue sniffing', 'Theft', 'Assault';
no flying furniture or angry doors;
no mad binge drinking, pills, gang fights. Best thing
that ever happened, changed him overnight.

It's all on show: iconic photographs;
Dress uniform, fresh pressed, back of the door;
'Day the whole town turned out' the headline news.
In pride of place, with words like 'bravery,
freedom, duty beyond the call, hard blow',
handwritten letter, framed, from his CO.

MICHAEL BRETT

Bomb Attack

The first pass is invisible.
Its slipstream can make a rock of the head
In a Turner seascape.
The bird, death, wanders the domes from ear to ear,
Sometimes deafening them;
Sometimes making them bleed.

Sometimes, it just lands.
Then, its stillness amazes you.
The fringes flickering over plastic eyes,
Amongst the corkscrew smoke and sirens.
It makes sparrows of men, men of sparrows.

Sparrows don't want to die, either.
They paddle as fast as they can,
Away from the sparrowhawk death,
Whose wings are a shadow over the sun.

Bomb Circuitry

Consider the circuitry of a bomb. Like you
It works with a telephone call.

A circuit board has political independence.
It has its own batteries, its own power.
It is as pretty and clever as a tube map.
Its parts are ancient books and modern coins.

A bomber is an artist, an electric surrealist
Who sees towers as gibbets, forests as fish bones.
On the black print of his newspaper, he solders
Semtex to gold, timers to copper.

He can write in the smoke over cars and buildings,
Sketch with the trails of planes and speedboats.
He can arrange death like a tub of flowers in the street
As a work of art, a Goya bullfight with bands and costumes.

The Entry Of Osama Bin Laden Into Paradise

Imagine that it exists, and that he travels there,
The bright warrior star, the meteor
Climbing forever up a rainbow reputation:

At his hands, at his feet are angels one-five at angels one-five.
Their singing unravels death's mysteries and its stillness,
Causes the dead to wake, to swarm like bees
Outnumbering all the living.
There are so many dead.

Their waking voices gasp and echo in Heaven's pyramid hives.
Some spill into its cavernous, rumouring streets,
Death's if-onlys and its might-have-beens.

Some, the more restless dead, sit astride Heaven's
Terracotta rooftops, its Chinese warrior horses.

They stare upwards at Heaven's runway,
Unrolling like a famous tongue to meet him

From Sirius to Polaris, their hands sway like anemones
On coral reefs. They lift their children so he can see them:

So many dead.
So many dead.

Feeding The War Gods In This Age Of Miracles

I've come back to the battlefield for the memorial service.

Today, the dead names chime like antique clocks
All set at different times.

The blue riflemen shoulder arms and walk away,
Leaving us to live on through this time of careless miracles
Where the dead can speak to us through DVDs and screens
As carelessly as the sun reflects itself on water.
They age only as old phone books do, in their usefulness to us.

Here, where days once straggled through barbed wire yards
Sharpened by fear and shaped by death –
The spring trees shout with blossom
And the cat sunshine rolls against memorials, graves;

Below the winged mosaic of clouds,
The Arabic script of holiday jets
Where birdsong shines, there calls the simple horn.
Goodbye.

Now, back in my hotel room, I call upon you all –
Old friends – to press your hands to your sides of the mirror
So that mine can cover yours, thus
Feeding the war gods in this age of miracles.

Machine Gun

He is a conjuror.
His bullets are birds' eggs.
He cloaks the theatre in his magic smoke.
He mesmerises people. He cuts ladies in half.
Encamped, wind–battered in a tent
Of flesh, I carry him and his boxes as he tours.
I watch his stars with nets of bad luck
Trawl the world.
Each day is an argument, a museum we fight for.
Sleep is three hours in a dust–filled bath
Under some noseless statues.
Beneath the awning of a marble hand,
I contemplate my future and my maps.
The colours of the nations are rich as bruises.
Roads are red veins. My conjuror has scissors.
He cuts the air.
He cuts us all.
He makes people disappear.

Mosques And Rockets

Daily life can only bark in backyards at the stars,
But rockets and mosques point in the same direction:
Counting down in Arabic.

They are both clean as needles.
Both stare up at stars painted on Moorish lattice work
Or ceilings of wood or perspex. At dawn, they
Stand and steam, are horses bridled by mathematics,
Saddled by astronomy. We can lie and steal,
Make compromises and say 'That's the way Life is'.
But rocket motors call like Mullahs from the skies.
Their flames are things once seen only in Greek speculation,
Dactyls or swirls of Arabic. For both, Zero and Hazaan times
Are blast-offs. Perhaps both are Jihads for the merciful.

US and Russian astronauts, Sufis, see in the curves of moons,
The same fragile curves that cup the thoughts in human skulls.
All these float between worlds. Above the clouds
The earth is their flexed symposium, a spherical table
Where they pour out thoughts like hot tea into glasses.

Suicide Bomber

I became a Buckingham Palace guide for death.
I timed my transformation to the instant (8.51)
I climbed aboard a Piccadilly Line train.
Look, admire death's portraits and its corridors.
Over its flowers I would rearrange the flowers of yourselves
In the vases of your bodies.

My bones were an embroidery of the air.
This was no loss of life but a culmination.
My body was a set of mosaic pieces destined for this instant.
My violence, a kind of art, a dream language, like music
Something scribbled in the surprised air.

When it subsided – my ragged portrait –
The Police and the Army were my tourists.
They entered, looked around, took photographs
And spoke in hushed tones.
I had blessed the train with reverence.
I am the man with no head and a bar of chocolate.

London, my home, was attacked by suicide bombers on 7th of July 2005.

9/11 Poem from London:
Tomorrow It Will All Run Backwards

Tomorrow, it will all run backwards.

The steel tsunamis will froth back upwards
And become solid.
The planes will be pulled out like javelins
And slide backwards, swallowing their vapour trails.

Tomorrow, everyone will be fine.

Tomorrow, everyone who died will come home.
They will sit again at the tables of home
And rejoin life's fellowship, its snapshots, tea
And picnics.

Tomorrow, all will be well.

Everyone will sleep as babies do under mobiles,
Untroubled by strange sounds, of aero engines
Flying too low and shadows over the streets.

Tomorrow, mobile phones will be just toys again.
The sky will be clear, blue, unbroken.

CHARLIE BROWN

They Gave Me A Medal

I returned from the Gulf, I'd changed in myself,
There was something not right, affected my health.
I'd been part of a killing, that didn't seem right,
But they gave me medal, for my part in the fight.
They honoured my actions, for fulfilling their plan,
But I'm not like I was, I'm not the same man.
It's easy to kill, become mad and insane,
It's not easy to live, with the torment and pain.
The enemy killed, they couldn't win if they tried,
But I must still fight, the enemy inside.
So this medal they gave me, for the role I played,
Was for part of the killing of thousands we slayed.
Well that makes me feel good, my stomach can settle,
My reward for my actions, was some moulded metal.
Well I'm sorry, it just seems, there's something I lack.
Instead of the medal, my life, I want back...

JB BROWN

A Reckoning

Flying over the Potomac
And away from the heart
Of the American Dream, was
Like crossing the Rubicon.
There was no turning back.

The shadowed hope of an ally,
And dreams of our glory and history,
Beckon, but do not deny
The fragility of adventure.

The creature of memory
Holds a picture which depreciates
All happiness, all fear.

And in the heat; acceptance,
Whilst the lights burn bright at home.

And in the bloody dust; redemption.

Do Not Hesitate

'The god of war hates
Those who hesitate.'*
But he hates the vanquished more.
Not for him the dishonourable and weak,
But the chosen, the glorious fallen and the victor.

When you see one thousand leopards
Storming from the sun,
You know you are in Valhalla,
And somehow your luck went wrong;
The bullet, the IED, the rocket,
The child suicide bomber.

Not for the soldier is luxury.
Only the choice to pull the trigger,
To take the next step on unsafe terrain,
To look for the enemy,
To choose to save a life,
To choose to take one.

Do not hesitate soldier.
It could be your last mistake.
Your reward would be expiration and enmity
Of the god of war,
For he hates the indecisive.

Quote taken from Euripides.

God Allows An Angel To Die

It was Tuesday.
A heart stopped
At the end of your phone call.
It was so sudden.

Behind a rage of windows
A sea of faces
Prayed for your descent.
Just before the collapse
Of what we all knew.

I saw no wings
Snapshot man,
During your angel fall.

Judgement Has Found You Worthy

Hold fast,
The King of Kings has spoken.
Hold fast when you fight your gods,
Your monsters and windmills,
Just like Don Quixote.

When your sorrowful tear falls upon
The scars of the last wound or death,
And you cannot see for blurred, devastated vision,
Leave no man behind.

When you walk with the bold,
In certain knowledge,
Hold fast for you're the dying proof of sacrifice.

Your bleeding side parallels another,
And crying will not save you.

Hold fast and you will have a beautiful grave.

Of The Oleander

There is one blade of grass
Growing on your grave,
In the dust from 1941.
The gunner on your right –
A howitzer man,
The pilot on your left –
He once flew into the sun.
Both fell when the attacks came in.

The verandahs now lie in disarray,
Trees unkempt, the troops long gone.
Rutted roads lead to the missing epitaphs,
Which read like a message from the dead,
'Here we lie, not the first, not the last,
Defiled in a broken land.'

In Habbaniyah,
The *Nerium* wept oleandrin and neriine poison
Whilst the *muntahik hurmat el kibor*
Desecrated the graves
Of your Abyssinian comrades.

The dust is still on Armistice Day,
It is heavy on the ground,
Despite the breeze,
Which once fanned
The soldiers and airmen
Of the Oleander.

Armistice Ceremony, Habbaniyah, Iraq,
11 November 2008.

Stealing Stars

When the maelstrom strikes,
With you laden of hope,
And it holds you fixed
Pray for courage and salvation.

A cold headstone.
In the middle of France,
Or the heat of the empire,
Or a forgotten field,
Or in the cool green of home,
Because the King of Kings
Has spoken.

And taken you away
And stolen a star.

The Availability Of The Dead

And there was an equal amount of pain.
As everybody was available.

But the line was short.
It was all based on supposition,
In order to formulate a gathering
Of the definitive, soon available dead.

They walked through ploughed field,
They traipsed through bone.
They were smashed and shattered.
And formed a collective show.

How to fight desperate tears?
When presence means nothing to the ghosts.
How to say hello to the dead?
Who are available in droves.

The Baghdad Cigar Aficionado Club

The Baghdad Cigar Aficionado Club
Always starts with a prayer
For families, for hope
And then for the brethren.
Later, there is silent recognition of
The sudden explosion beyond our walls
And the firefight flashes on the horizon.

Overhead, the medevac helos
Always sound angry, especially at night,
Engines roaring a protest
Against the misery of their cargo,
As they fly to their grim sanctuary of hope,
With crewmen full of purpose and pity.

At the Baghdad Cigar Aficionado Club,
Many wish the leaf they burn
Was the causal afterglow
Of those distant firefights,
As the aromatic smoke drifts
Upward, toward the rotor wash,
Laden with unspoken gratitude that
They, are in a safe camaraderie, and
The medevac crews are not, for now,
Mopping up their blood.

Baghdad, 11 October 2008.

With acknowledgement to Prince Sined Yar Maharg of fabled Xanadu.

The Battle List & The Way Ahead

I would like to have seen
The fights at the Marne, Delville Wood, Beaumont Hamel,
And the last great cavalry battle of Meggido,
In all their heroic, tragic glory
As long as I survived.

And all of the others; the inexhaustible list.
The Somme, Sangin, Singapore,
Isandlwana, Basrah, Lucknow, Vimy Ridge
The Crimea, Musa Qala, Waterloo,
Goose Green, Rorke's Drift, Kajaki Dam,
Normandy, Ortona, Al Amarah, Zungeni Mountain,
The Rhine Crossing, Ypres, Hong Kong, Habbaniyah.

A few of many. Say enough of them
And the metronomic effect
Dulls the pain. Strengthens resolve.
Harkens to glory; in defeat or victory.

The battle list is long my friend, but
It is longer for the dead,
And it is not over yet.
For by example, we lead.

Germany, July 2009.

The Boneyard

The Boneyard at Taji
Holds the detritus of war.
Lost and dangerous toys, skeletons
Seeking their previous owners,
Whose stories are embedded
In the rusting metal,
Just as metal was embedded
In them.

If only the silent hulks
Could speak of the
Interior terror, the sweat,
Of glad hails of fleeting victory,
And the darkness and
Sporadic tracer light,
Before their own demise.

Burnt and scoured by the sun,
The messages of aftermath
Are written on their sides,
With a graffiti of love,
Hope and comedy.
But the broken toys
Would weep if they could,
The same as their ancestors
At Normandy and El Alamein.
And they would speak of fragility
And honour,
And furious pain.

Taji and Baghdad, 21-23 October 2008.

The Conservation Of Angular Momentum

If you lined the Appian Way
With the souls on crosses
Of all of our dead soldiers,
And had the widows grieving
At their spectral feet,
What a monument to God it would be;
A multitude replica of Golgotha.

Is it hubris to think
There is poetry in the slaying of enemies,
But there is no respite from lust ?
For everywhere there are reminders
Of fragility and mortality,
Of paradise lost and of a desert Masterma
And a tornado of fallen men,
Reaching, arms outstretched
Into an empty sky.

The Great Debate

Entrée

Churchill said,
'We must defeat evil.'
And Jesus agreed.

Ghandi said,
'But it must be achieved peacefully.'
Hope agreed.

Kofi said,
'Of course, but, this must be debated.'
Conan disagreed.

He said,
'In battle, valour is all,
And the lamentations of the women mean victory.'

But on the day Wilfred Owen died,
Siegfried cried,
And the table sat in silence.

The Main Course

Vera said,
'We'll meet again.'
Tommy disagreed.

'My friends are dead,'
He said.
And God agreed.

He said,
'So is my son, and the fault is mine.'
Futility agreed.

Faith retorted,
'Good may come of this.'
And Mohammed went to the mountain,

But the mountain maintained
Neutrality.
And never spoke.

Dessert
Jesus rose and opened the tomb.
Torquemada opened discussion,
And nobody disagreed.

Then dessert was served,
It was truly exquisite, delightfully sweet,
Conversation lulled.

Après
After dinner, talk resumed.
As smoke curled and swam
Amongst the old wood beams,
And the fumes from an excellent year
Dulled the senses.
A remark was heard,
'Enough talk, it is time for action.'

The silent four horsemen,
Reluctant guests,
Grinned.
'We agree,' they said.

The Promise Of Things To Come

Hüzün haunts me,
It rises impatient,
Weaving inside my heart,
Calling to my soul.

Only the foolish desire,
Moments of frantic fear, amongst
Shards, flying almost by instinct,
Hissing, spitting furious
Flechettes and heat
Shedding copper-jacketed poison,
Inverting and shredding the air.

Who would choose such a fate ?
With nothing to show
But memories of pain,
A glint of hanging metal
Broken fragments of triumph,
And only blood to slake the serpent,
With the promise of things to come.

Baghdad, 7 October 2008.

Where Your Ashes Kiss The Earth

At the end, a flag and your medals,
And a salute, brother.
Perhaps, there will be
An Enochian song,
A welcoming on high.
For you. One of our own.

In glacial millennia,
We are as naught but dust
After our halcyon days;
Carefree, lustful and invincible,
With the energy of the sun.
But in a thousand years,
Where your ashes kiss the earth,
Perhaps you will be remembered
As a man amongst men.
But no more so than now,
As we weep with your widow.

Perhaps our mute sorrow will
Be salute enough for you, friend,
And the wild savagery that follows
Your sombre burning, will be
Our keening of gratitude,
For one of our own.

Baghdad, 23 December 2008.

Dedicated to my friend, Lt Col Neil Lewis RLC, CO 27 Regt RLC. Died 23 Dec 2008 of cancer. He deserved better.

KATIE BUTLER-MANUEL

War

The ceaseless gunfire in the night,
The screams of dying men,
Forever echo in my head,
The noise goes round and round

The dawn across the battlefields,
The eerie blood-red light,
The bodies of the fallen,
Haunt me day and night,
My comrades lie forgotten,
No funeral wake for them
Lost in a futile war
When will we ever learn?

DANIEL CLAYTON

Tour Of Duty

Heat, dust, sun and sand,
Patrolling through Helmand rifle in hand.

Searing heat, sun up high,
This job is tough they would not lie.

IEDs, bullets and guns,
This dangerous mix, it isn't fun.

A far-flung land, miles from home,
Once a week, they can pick up a phone.

They tell their loved ones it's okay,
And to understand it's just a short stay.

They hang up the phone and say goodbye,
As tracer arcs through midnight sky.

They are scared; they lie in fear,
Sensing their enemy is drawing near.

They engage the enemy by returning fire,
Unfortunately situations can be dire.

Then radio the helicopters above their heads;
Just to make sure the enemy have fled.

End of tour is not that far,
As they dream of that flight out of Kandahar.

Back to home, they leave their base;
They can honestly say they hate that place.

Soldiers marching in column of route,
They halt sharply and final salute.

End of tour medals are awarded,
Smiles and laughter, as families applauded.

A moment's silence, the pipers sound,
And quietly remember, those not around.

A comrade gone is never lost;
All soldiers are familiar with the ultimate cost.

They don't want pity, or anyone to sob,
Remember instead, they love their job.

Soldiers are selfless and fiercely proud;
They serve their country because they're allowed.

MARTIN CROWSON

A Soldier's Battle Thought

'Forward Men' a sergeant cried,
As we hurried from trenches filled with water,
My closest friends were by my side,
As we raced into that night of slaughter.
Mortars explode and shots ring out,
But we keep on going weary and tired.
Bodies dropping all about,
From enemies' bullets they have fired.

My mind right now begins to wander,
Thinking of my family, relations and friends,
Trying to block out, the roar and thunder,
Of bombs that drop without no ends.
My mother, father, wife and son,
Will I be alive when this war ends?
I've come to fight 'What have I done?'
To leave my comfort of home and friends.

Back to reality, and all this noise,
Men, injured, dying all around me.
'Look! There goes another of our boys!',
I call! as a bullet rips into my knee.
Now down I go in blood and pain,
And my foe, above his gun I face.
He points it down, and shoots again,
So now I leave, this fight for race.

All goes black, my life I see,
All goes quiet, as wife leaves me.
I never thought that I would die,
As I heard that sergeant's 'forward' cry.

JO De VRIES

Valentine From Kabul

You came to me today in a mirage,
your face nearly melted in memory.
You were a strange sight amidst this barrage
of snow and sand assaulting the city.
I waited for you to speak of our life,
but you were carried away in a crush
of the walking dead, whose anger and strife
have opened a divide between us.

Here, the world readies itself for an end
that I fear may come to purge this forsaken
land, laying waste to all that we defend.
If this happens I may well be taken.

You must know, I fight so you are free of
fear and death, barricaded forever by love.

(for Capt. L.G.)

GEORGE DOUGLAS

A Mother's Soldier Comes Home

A mother's soldier came home today.
Not to a fanfare welcome but to flags quietly
dipped in honour and the muted bugle call.
Through the town, subdued in welcome, you journey.
And as you leave a mother casts a rose with love and despair.
But it, unknowningly, slipped from your cold fingers
and lies alone in the wake of your passing.
The warm red petals fading in the soft quiet tears of the falling rain.
A mother's soldier came home today.

STEVEN FIRKINS

Art Of War

The sky's so light as the sun shines bright.
But darkness is around us, we feel its might,
Tanks and guns in all their awe,
Fighting and killing they all want more.
Notches and nicks in a blade,
Funny how the measure of life is made.
Intelligence is high and weapons are smart,
But blue on blue still ruins the art.
With the human factor mistakes take place,
Killing maiming our friendly face.
Flames raise high and rumble spreads wide,
Engulfing towns in a deep dark tide.
Oil burns fuels are used,
For metal monsters to abuse.
Do they hear the crying the screaming,
Or is it just bad dreaming?
Helmets and body armour weapons held with pride,
Webbing and bergans for the long homeward ride.
Forgetting the cause but not what they saw,
With pride and honour in the art of war.

Afghanistan 2006.

Brotherhood

Even though I've suffered more hardships than gains
Found more kinship than love
I'd rather have had five minutes in a select brotherhood of men
Than an empty life of civilian ease
For the men and bosses I've meet through the years have a timeless bond
Of understanding and fellowship that can't be bored to tears
For every man feels some inadequacy for himself
Never having served for Queen and Country or even having stepped in the
shadowed boots of old
Stand and fight as one
To ensure the timeless History so the Squadron Brotherhood can live on.

Ode to 51 Para Squadron.

Cross The Line

Awaiting the move to cross the line,
To fight and protect for peace of mind.
To clear the way for the rest to follow,
Through death and pain we all feel sorrow.
For time is borrowed so we work hard,
Fighting playing on dealt cards.
It soon ends and we go to our homes,
Telling stories of men's laid bones.

Distant Peace

Another sun rises on a distant land,
Browns greens yellows make it look so bland.
But then our metal monsters scar the ground,
Pepper-potting leap-frogging bound by bound.
With worried distant stares from young and old,
Tired shameful glances from those being bold.
Hearts and minds with long hand-shakes,
Quiet whispers in the background and the peace breaks.
Tea down with looks of sorrow,
With a knowing grimace it starts again tomorrow.

Afghanistan 2010.

Queen And Country

If I die whilst doing my job,
Would Queen and country sob?
Is this fight a lost cause,
Or is it simple a violent pause?
If we were told we were about to die,
Would even the strongest cry?
People say fight for the homeland,
Do our lives hold such little demand.
People urge us on to fight,
How do they know this conflict's right?
Conscience should hold its own,
Does this feud jeopardise the throne?
Fanatics lay your weapons down,
Or face the wrath of the crown.
If you doubt or shun this threat,
Your lives will be at our nation's debt.
Queen and country just a song,
Or a petty feud gone wrong.

The End

The end has come and we sit still,
Adrenalin seeping from our will.
The conflict short but still bold
For the short fight took its toll.
We rest now and start to sleep,
Waiting for the alarm to beep.
It doesn't come our rest is tense,
Body and mind can't make sense.
The enemy's gone now we help,
To try to ease the guilt we felt.
Now we wait for the bird of love,
To carry us home this isn't no dove.
My weapon my kit then myself,
Now it's done let's spend our wealth.
Ale flows and the chorus rolls on,
The night won't finish until the end of the song.
Our minds now closed but the thought's still there,
We will remember their chests won't be bare.
They fought well and died as men,
Have no fear of thought 'WE WILL REMEMBER THEM'.

The Night

The sky is dark but the wind still roams,
We're far away from our near-forgotten homes.
The night is vast and all around,
Feels like being swallowed by the deep dark ground.
The air is creepy and full of fright,
But we must stand tall strong with might.
We can't see them but we know they're there,
Standing pointing with a long strange stare.
Our bodies tense and full of heat,
For the work tomorrow will break its beat.
We ache and hurt but will not weep,
For we all look forward to a deep dark sleep.

Afghanistan 2006.

Welcome To The Valley

Boom Boom Valhalla's calling
Mortar bombs are doing there mulling
A nice welcome to Sangin Valley
We're all bombed up and looking ally
Duck and run from place to place
Helmets and body armour is the case
Dig in here and sandbag there
Stick against the Hesco to avoid their stares
A volley of fire a salvo out bound
They're not even fazed they keep to their rounds
Warnings here handshakes there
And still we comeback with one spare
The gloves are off we're here to win
Hearts and minds and infiltrate within
You're on your back foot now we all can see
So let's scratch this one up to a big V
Bring them all, make sure you rally
Cos it's our turn to welcome you to the valley.

CLEVELAND W. GIBSON

Dear Husband

The dreams I have of you are nightmares filled with
war-sounds, also light so like the blinding red of
sunsets, and the deep blue-greens of the sea.

How I miss you, Dear Husband, where on my awaking
nothing changes, life is slow, it shuffles on its way,
sunshine enters, brings slight relief, a small smile but it never ever stays.

Now, I gasp as I've seen your shadow, hanging on
the wall. Nailed to it I see once again glory, Iraq,
Afghanistan and all. And in there lies a bayonet, a
grenade, a George Cross too, and free-flying the
Union flag: the red, the white, and blue.

You are my brave soldier you gave the world your
best, unable to forget those days of blood-torn terror,
and sweat upon your vest.

You who know that the brave don't ever run, but they
stop or rather stay, counting out precious minutes, as
those minutes make up a day.

People look to find a hero. To me you are my one. I know
every soldier is somebody's brother, father, uncle or son.

My tears never stop nor my heartaches fade away,
and so I pick up your medal you won on that special day.

My fingers stroke and cherish, I'll wear it with pride.
It is part of what I have of you forever by my side.

Old Soldier

As I grow old I notice
the days talk to me. All
stand for good times
yet some need
sympathy. Monday
comes to talk of new
things or perhaps, to
steer my way. Then
Tuesday will usher in a
simple idea, alas, one I
know must stay.
Wednesday is like a
sweet child but
Thursday spells out a
treat. But unlucky
Friday's rants about
number thirteen, a
curse that leads to
Hell. Maybe we'll all
end up there, but who
can ever really tell?
The lively months leap
by so fast they make
me blink. Julius
Caesar's death in
March, now that makes
me think. June: I
sweat, August: I
quiver. Sweet
December: rock-hard
ice, no time to sail the
river. When years pass
without a word, and a
Birthday card arrives
from the Queen. My
jaw drops, bowled.

IVOR GURNEY

Strange Hells

There are strange Hells within the minds war made
Not so often, not so humiliating afraid
As one would have expected – the racket and fear guns made.

One Hell the Gloucester soldiers they quite put out;
Their first bombardment, when in combined black shout
Of fury, guns aligned, they ducked low their heads
And sang with diaphragms fixed beyond all dreads,
That tin and stretched-wire tinkle, that blither of tune;
'Après la guerre fini' till Hell all had come down,
Twelve-inch, six-inch, and eighteen-pounders hammering Hell's thunders.

Where are they now on State-doles, or showing shop patterns
Or walking town to town sore in borrowed tatterns
Or begged? Some civic routine one never learns.
The heart burns – but has to keep out of face how heart burns.

Chosen by Gwyn Roberts.

STEVE HALLIWELL

What Makes A Hero's Road

Walking down the road one day my rifle in my hand,
Ahead another squaddie, his boots all covered in sand.
He must be from a desert post, like me a dusty wreck,
God the sand gets everywhere, and the sun it burns your neck.

It's strange there is just two of us walking side by side,
I'm having trouble looking back, but believe me I have tried.
The tiredness of these last few months, heavy though it's been,
As we walk along this road it seems a distant dream.

Soon a friend called out to me 'Welcome home, my boy',
And as I looked there's loads of girls crying tears of Joy.
Then a voice from my past 'Your battles are all done',
'Come and join the rest of us and leave behind your gun'.

But those tears weren't of joy, and wreaths they do abound,
Now I hear my mother's voice and it's a far far different sound.
The voice of Grandad was who I'd heard, dead these many years,
And there, he's standing, waiting, so I wipe away the tears.

I've done my tour, my battles are done, I did as I was asked,
I manned the walls, dug the ditches, so often was I tasked.
Now others come to take my place, for them it's oh so new,
And they will give, all they can, because that's what we do.

We'll give our lives if needed, as soldiers that's our trade,
For battlefields across the world is where our game is played.
But then we need a road to walk to meet those gone before,
Grandad who died in WW1 and his dad who fought the Boer.

I've heard old soldiers talk of roads, the last that they shall tread,
A road that only soldiers walk and angels wait ahead.
A road that's fit for heroes, at the closing of the day,
A place where friends can gather, to wish you on your way.

JODIE HENDERSON

Lone Chimes

People lined up by the roadside,
As the church bell rang out loud,
The lone chimes for the soldier
Remembered by the crowd.

The cortege drove by with honour,
Flags and heads bowed in unity,
Respect for his ultimate sacrifice,
Was present for all around me.

The grief of the people,
The emotion of the day,
I couldn't continue taking photographs
Couldn't capture the pain this way.

The silence was overwhelming,
I didn't want to cry,
I found it so unbearable,
Witnessing a family's goodbye.

A stranger passed me a tissue,
She notices my upset,
That day in Wootton Bassett
I will never forget.

STEVEN LESLIE HILL

Foot Patrol

Hot dry dust
Under a burning sun
Our foot patrol
Has just begun

Walking along in a
Random file
The locals watch us
Without a smile

We know they are here
'intelligence' tells us so
It seems they are going
To make a show

Rifle at the ready
Safety catch off
My eyes now focused
On the roofs aloft

Body armour and helmet
Seem to weigh a ton
With dry-mouthed anticipation
I'm scoping my gun

Suddenly a bang
And confusion ahead
As hot metal shrapnel
Flies over our heads

There is 'incoming' now
From the roofs above
'Rounds' kick the dust
With a whine and a thud

The 'firefight's' on
Adrenalin's high
As another explosion
Rocks the sky

Our returning fire
The 'rounds' hit home
Ripping into roof parapets
Plaster and stone

We know they took
'Hits' and are now away
Afghanistan with the 'Paras'
It's just another day

TJ HODGETTS

Dressing The Dead

Two bodies lay before me:
Who they are I cannot tell.
Flesh charred by an explosion,
Gives a sweet and sickly smell.

A mortar round has landed
On the internet welfare shack,
And roasted both *in situ*
As they e-mailed family back.

Their faces have been melted,
No dog-tags round their necks,
Only bits of clothing remnants
To help I.D. by the Med Techs.

Their limbs have all contracted,
Twisted postures fixed in death.
As we force their legs out straight,
Exhaled bubbles mimic breath.

My arms are caked in charcoal
From where they've rubbed on skin.
My desert boots are soiled with blood
And destined for the bin.

The indignity's completed:
Bodies bound and sealed in bags.
The cold *Grim Reefer** names the souls
With 'Male, large, unknown' tags.

Two medics are affected
By what they've seen and done.
I counsel them as I am numbed
With wounds from bomb and gun.

*This poem refers to the unenviable task that falls to medical staff at the field hospital of examining the dead for legal diagnosis and International Death Certificate purposes. *Grim Reefer is the name given to the refrigerated ISO container (or 'reefer') that is used as a temporary mortuary.*

Sangin Valley

Fifty feet above the ground,
Spewing seven-point-six-two lead,
Banks to fool a MANPAD firer:
Bullets split the Taliban's head.

RPG, nine-hundred yards,
The safety fuse will make charge blow,
Good job it is bloody hard,
Predicting where the chopper goes.

SAM locked-on: cock-pit alarm,
Chaff and flares burst out her tail.
Turns and dives to avoid harm,
Helpless freight looks sick and pale.

Higher up, two-thousand feet,
Apache views the threat on ground:
Hellfire sends the beard to meet
Allah with an explosive sound.

Screaming up the Sangin valley,
Twin rotors drag the heavy bird.
Small rounds chase the flight in volleys,
Each Kevlar 'ping' by aircrew heard.

The landing zone's a poppy field,
Brown scored heads in down-draught sway.
It's a paradox that this crop's yield,
Could take our soldiers' pain away.

Enemy fire strafes the aircraft,
The Quick Reaction Force deploys.
Mini-gun puffs its metal hatred,
The patients' pleas are drowned in noise.

As if on a giant bungee,
We lurch again into the sky.
On our knees we offer comfort,
To limbless comrades as they die.

Oil pressure is reducing;
Hydraulic system has been hit.
No 'comms' for medics means that nothing,
Is known of a potential ditch.

Chinook returns to Bastion:
Human cargo sighs relief.
A little battle has been won –
Some relatives denied of grief.

Written in Afghanistan in 2007 while the author was part of the helicopter-borne Medical Emergency Response Team (MERT): this team flies to the point of wounding in a Chinook helicopter to provide advanced medical care to soldiers en route to the field hospital.

Glossary
MANPAD: a shoulder launched weapon system
SAM: Surface to Air Missile
7.62mm: the caliber of general purpose machine gun bullets
RPG: Rocket Propelled Grenade
Kevlar: armour plating
Mini-gun: machine gun firing 1000 rounds per minute, mounted on helicopter

Solifugit

Brown and hairy,
Very scary,
If a spider phobia you've got.
Anaesthetic,
She injects it,
To numb your skin (I kid you not).
In your shadow,
She will follow,
To keep herself out of the sun.
You may well fear,
As she draws near,
You are being chased and you must run.
Solifugit,
Camel spider,
Arachnid urban myths abound.
'As big as plates!';
'It ate my face!';
'It jumped six feet right off the ground!'
In a mess tin,
With a scorpion,
(Heat the tin over a flame).
Soldiers will bet,
On *Solifugit*,
To triumph in this lethal game.

Written in Afghanistan, 2007, while deployed as a Consultant in Emergency Medicine in the British field hospital at Camp Bastion.

The Camel Spider is not actually a spider, but a member of the genus Solifugae. *They look like spiders, but will hide from the sun (hence their name) and run into your shadow. If you move, they will follow your shadow, giving the impression they are chasing you!*

Death Of A Clock

Tick-tock
Sprawled on our camp cots
Tick-tock
Beneath our fly nets
Tick-tock
The tent is airless
Tick-tock
I wouldn't care less
If you'd shut up that ticking clock!

Tick-tock
Each night I'm woken
Tick-tock
To tend bodies broken
Tick-tock
I can't do my best
Tick-tock
If I've had no rest
So shut up that bloody clock!!

Tick-tock
I've lost perspective
Tick-tock
To live and let live
Tick-tock
There's one solution
Bang! Bang!
It's execution
Of that fucking ticking clock!!!

Written in Afghanistan, 2007, while deployed as a Consultant in Emergency Medicine in the British field hospital at Camp Bastion.

Amputee

Is he less of a man
Missing legs, amputated?
Compensation a sham:
Only one limb's been rated.

By the pains from his stumps
Every night he is woken.
He cries out, his hand held:
Nursing words softly spoken.

New prosthetics displace
Old aesthetics and should
Give more function than Ace
Pilots' legs of hard wood.

They don't want your pity,
Your uncomfortable smiles.
War's children aren't pretty
But they're proud and alive.

Can he go back to work
With one eye or one hand?
Fly a desk as a clerk
Or will this be too bland?

Will he hanker for action
Red tape will deny?
Will hope turn to rancour
Will he no longer try?

Will a Purple Heart open
A jar or a tin
Or a door to a job
A more able man's in?

Will his girlfriend stick by him
Or marry from guilt?
Can she live with burns scarring,
A face to rebuild?

In two years he returns
To wards where he lay
New wife on his good arm
Big smile on his face.

To raw comrades fearful
Their lives are destroyed
This champion of hope
Is bitterness devoid.

Written in Afghanistan, 2007, while deployed as a Consultant in Emergency Medicine in the British field hospital at Camp Bastion. The compensation for serious combat injuries has been enhanced since this poem was written.

A Hymn For Helmand

(To the tune of 'Melita')

For all those soldiers in Helmand
Who sacrificed their lives, we stand
To honour each one's memory
And pray that each one's soul is freed.
    Let every soldier hear you say:
    'We value what you do today.'

For all those soldiers in Helmand
Whose blood was shed and stained the sand;
Who lost their limbs or lost their mind,
We'll help them heal and peace to find.
    Let every soldier hear you say:
    'We value what you do today.'

For all those soldiers in Helmand
Who live through war to understand
The horror and brutality
Of taking life for liberty.
    Let every soldier hear you say:
    'We value what you do today.'

Written in Afghanistan, 2009, while Medical Director of the combined British, Danish and American field hospital at Camp Bastion.

DEAN HORTON

The Airborne Medic's Creed

I will go toe to toe with the Angel of Death;
I will use every weapon at my disposal to defeat him.
I will remain tuned to the highest level at all times,
And my skills shall never fade –
For me knowledge and courage will bring about victory.
Through adversity I will never falter,
And on wings of healing I will carry you through the darkness.

IAN JOLLEY & MICHAEL MALIN

Wife, Friend, Lover

We join the Army to the see the world,
More often than not the conditions are bad,
To march through countries with flags unfurled.
A sunshine tour is not happy but usually sad.
Exciting tours to some strange land,
Sometimes it may seem we don't miss you that much,
In rain and sun, through snow and sand.
One or two letters, hardly keeping in touch.

The Forces together, pulling as one,
Remember that sometimes we are rushed off our feet,
Our reputation always second to none,
Out all day patrolling down some dusty street.
Comrades in arms, friends one and all,
Locked in a vehicle, surrounded by steel
If we are ever in need they will hear our call.
Please just imagine how lonely that must feel.

The home fires still burning, support from afar,
Birthdays are missed as well as Christmas Day,
Our families are with us, wherever we are.
Not seeing our children grow up and play.
Remaining at home staying strong and true,
Soldering on through thick and thin,
When we are apart they suffer too.
With strength and support from you, we will always win.

Our time away is always hard,
There are good times and bad times across the years,
Our lives in danger always seem to be on our guard.
Laughter and happiness and sometimes tears,
Training can help us prepare for the worst,
You suffer as we do, but grow stronger each day.
The British Armed Forces forever coming first.
Life in the Forces has always been this way.

You may think we have fun when we are away,
Sunshine is fine when you are in a bar,
We do work hard, but find time to play.
Not driving around in some armoured car,
A holiday it's not but we do our best,
Don't think that sand means we are on the beach,
Even a soldier needs his rest.
The sea is usually well out of arm's reach.

We thank you for your loyalty across the miles,
For your love and respect and all those smiles,
Remember one thing will always be true,
And so a heartfelt message from me to you...

You can be a soldier for the rest of your life,
But a man would be nothing without his girlfriend or wife.

Dedicated to the wives and girlfriends of all soldiers.

HENRY KEMPSTER

The Casualty

Open fire!
Yes! What does it mean?
Such death, maiming and destruction.

Slouching in a doorway, lots of blood.
Running and screaming all around,
but still he lay there.
Sanctuary against the wall, but for how long?
Leg is off and in so much pain.
Nowhere to go, soldiers are coming,
running is not an option.

The soldiers come, but deliberate to rescue.
Resources are low.
The Casualty is in pain, so much pain.
Decisions come slow,
feelings about war run high,
but the Casualty dies
and the Casualty was only nine.

RUDYARD KIPLING

The Young British Soldier

WHEN the 'arf-made recruity goes out to the East
'E acts like a babe an' 'e drinks like a beast,
An' 'e wonders because 'e is frequent deceased
Ere 'e's fit for to serve as a soldier.
Serve, serve, serve as a soldier,
Serve, serve, serve as a soldier,
Serve, serve, serve as a soldier,
So-oldier *of* the Queen!

Now all you recruities what's drafted to-day,
You shut up your rag-box an' 'ark to my lay,
An' I'll sing you a soldier as far as I may:
A soldier what's fit for a soldier.
Fit, fit, fit for a soldier ...

First mind you steer clear o' the grog-sellers' huts,
For they sell you Fixed Bay'nets that rots out your guts –
Ay, drink that 'ud eat the live steel from your butts –
An' it's bad for the young British soldier.
Bad, bad, bad for the soldier ...

When the cholera comes – as it will past a doubt –
Keep out of the wet and don't go on the shout,
For the sickness gets in as the liquor dies out,
An' it crumples the young British soldier.
Crum-, crum-, crumples the soldier ...

But the worst o' your foes is the sun over'ead:
You must wear your 'elmet for all that is said:
If 'e finds you uncovered 'e'll knock you down dead,
An' you'll die like a fool of a soldier.
Fool, fool, fool of a soldier ...

If you're cast for fatigue by a sergeant unkind,
Don't grouse like a woman nor crack on nor blind;
Be handy and civil, and then you will find
That it's beer for the young British soldier.
Beer, beer, beer for the soldier ...

Now, if you must marry, take care she is old –
A troop-sergeant's widow's the nicest I'm told,
For beauty won't help if your rations is cold,
Nor love ain't enough for a soldier.
'Nough, 'nough, 'nough for a soldier ...

If the wife should go wrong with a comrade, be loath
To shoot when you catch 'em – you'll swing, on my oath! –
Make 'im take 'er and keep 'er: that's Hell for them both,
An' you're shut o' the curse of a soldier.
Curse, curse, curse of a soldier ...

When first under fire an' you're wishful to duck,
Don't look nor take 'eed at the man that is struck,
Be thankful you're livin', and trust to your luck
And march to your front like a soldier.
Front, front, front like a soldier ...

When 'arf of your bullets fly wide in the ditch,
Don't call your Martini a cross-eyed old bitch;
She's human as you are – you treat her as sich,
An' she'll fight for the young British soldier.
Fight, fight, fight for the soldier ...

When shakin' their bustles like ladies so fine,
The guns o' the enemy wheel into line,
Shoot low at the limbers an' don't mind the shine,
For noise never startles the soldier.
Start-, start-, startles the soldier ...

If your officer's dead and the sergeants look white,
Remember it's ruin to run from a fight:
So take open order, lie down, and sit tight,
And wait for supports like a soldier.
Wait, wait, wait like a soldier ...

When you're wounded and left on Afghanistan's plains,
And the women come out to cut up what remains,
Jest roll to your rifle and blow out your brains
An' go to your Gawd like a soldier.
Go, go, go like a soldier,
Go, go, go like a soldier,
Go, go, go like a soldier,
So-oldier of the Queen.

Chosen by Iain McHenry.

JG MAGEE

High Flight

Oh, I have slipped the surly bonds of earth
and danced the skies on laughter-silvered wings.
Sunward I've climbed, and joined the tumbling
mirth of sun-split clouds, and done a hundred
things you have not dreamed of – wheeled
and soared and swung high in the sunlit silence.
Hov'ring there, I've chased the shouting wind along,
and flung my eager craft through footless halls of air.

Up, up, the long, delirious, burning blue,
I've topped the windswept heights with easy grace
where never lark, or even eagle flew.
And while with silent, lifting mind I've trod
the high untrespassed sanctity of space,
put out my hand, and touched the face of God.

September 3, 1941.

Chosen by John Nichol, Former RAF Pilot and Iraq Veteran.

PAUL MARLOW

Orphan

I am surrounded by loneliness, constantly
seeking that hidden element that seems
unobtainable, a part of myself lost.

My family gone, taken from me forcibly,
the worst of my life rolled into one and
disjointed throughout the years.

Jim, the cock-sure boisterous brother with
passion and flair, lying in my arms, broken,
shredded and bleeding.

Tom, the quiet one, a thinker, friend to all
that crossed his path. Huddled in piss,
stained red, pale white, frozen to the deck.

Steve, the optimist that gave us hope and shone
a light forward through the dark. Swinging lightly,
body slack, at the end of a rope.

Simon, the joker and dancing queen who
shattered the cloak of moroseness about us.
Alone, in a room bereft, with a pile of pills.

And what of me? Suicide glowers in the
shadow of my past. The gun is gone, my uniform
stripped away, I am locked out from a world

I called home, yet still tethered. The nightmare of
combat has never left me – my only source of
what it felt to be loved.

Rant

Sometimes I just want to fuck off,
away from this world, where thoughts
are conquered daily.

Mesmerised by a closed view, I want to
run, without a care for society's handbook,
served out to the masses.

Home into the fray of wild abandoned
hopes, chaotic structure and living on
the edge eating fear,

That place of hardened reality,
with simplistic choices and senses
honed to perfection,

Back in the carbon-laced smoke,
flying dirt and the familiar smell
of refined, cooked, gun oil.

Rapid Eye Movement

Tall black trees shoot straight up, dense dank bush in
knotted clumps and blue fog creeping by, in this ongoing
dream-state world. I run through the wood, my breath
heaves, pursued by a dark heavy grunting mass, close-in.

I break right to the cut-line of forest and earth. Stepping
over the boundary, a river runs like a snake slithering
through muddy banks and green leaf, its head gapes and
gags, spraying white gouts of venom.

A large oak stands singularly, guarding with twisted limbs
and stretched fingers, the solitary guardian of old.
A stabbing moan escapes its trunk and echoes across the void,
belching over me in waves of rotting vegetation.

She stands pale white against the browns, long silky strands
caress her face of mottled scars, eyes lost in shadowy regret,
a single tear slips silently from the rim and transgresses through
new-born buried flesh, pointing out into the abyss.

Friends float past, heads bobbing gently in the stream, soulless,
savaged relentlessly by the WAR machine, a mass of brutalised
metal and skin marching through fertile landscapes, harvesting
the vitality of our youth.

Split-Frame

I sit here and listen to words babble
through the intellectual maze, mouths
spraying letters. I'm torn between a

world of creativity and that of a
camouflaged cloak dipped in greens,
browns and blacks. They spill in fonts

of twelve, fourteen, sixteen, bold with
mixed metaphors and similes laced with
intent. Steeped in history, stringent rules,

rigid borders of what can be and cannot,
flood my head like a tide that slip silently
and secretly to the surface.

Men lost in the earth, faces marking their
distinction from that un-realised reality
of coldness, scorch my eyes and thoughts

through body and bone. A child walks into
focus, staggering in broken streets and
bombed out buildings, crying for his mother.

The bullets sing lullabies past my ears and
plough through his small body. He is down,
still, on the ground. Another faceless kid

brutally branded in my skull, as I struggle
sliding in old scars scabbed wet, through the
damp choking fog of things past.

NIGEL MARSHALL

Sleeping Out At Christmas

Winter has descended white on the hills above the town,
And below, are streets where shoppers browse, hunting bargains down,
Preparing for a Christmas time of food and drink and fun,
Forgetting those less fortunate, whom society will shun.
Neglected and alone he sleeps, wrapped up against the cold,
His belly filled with acidic beer or whiskey's fiery gold.
He remembers years when he too trod that route around the shops,
Buying up the trinkets and the tunes by next year's flops.

Those days are gone, so long ago; he lost them bit by bit,
He struggles with a world in which he feels he does not fit.
He saw so many things at war, which people should not see,
They stayed there in his mind, still now; they will not set him free,
How could he speak to those he loved and those he would protect,
Of his trauma and his helplessness as his mind was slowly wrecked?
Instead he sank into himself, withdrawn, so scared and tired.
Until eventually he lost it all and began his life outside.

He lost his wife, their kids, his job, because he couldn't cope,
He felt he had nowhere to turn; his mind destroyed his hope,
If you could only see the scenes which play inside his head,
Then you would understand sometimes he wishes he was dead.
It consumes all his energy and leaves him hollowed out,
And the silence of the freezing night is punctured by his shouts,
He wakes in shock, completely lost; not knowing what he's done,
But very quickly realises the old enemy has won.

This is how his mind has been for years and years and years,
It stalks him all through day and night and preys upon his fears,
Inside he craves understanding from those who hurry past,
But they just see a begging drunk, not worthy of their cash.
He'll drink it, sure. He has to do, to keep the cold at bay,
But he wishes that his mind would let him earn a good day's pay.
Instead it takes him back to war and shows his mates being killed,
This isn't what's supposed to be; it's not how it was billed.

A soldier's pride will hold him back from asking for a hand,
From those he paid his subs to, while marching to the band.
He gave his money willingly for the 'Boys of the Old Brigade'
But it's he who now needs charity, he now needs that aid.
Do not forget that this begging drunk, you pass on the other side,
Was once your willing protector, for you he would have died.
His mind was ripped to pieces by a war fought in your name,
Too many die on freezing streets – don't let him do the same.

Belfast, 2nd December 2008.

PAIGE McALWANE

Against The War

As hundreds of strangers line the street the bell in Wootton Bassett tolls,
Upon a silent town hundred strangers stand,
In full respect and support of soldiers who died in a foreign land.

An aircraft lands at Lyneham and brings the fallen home,
The funeral cortege will appear led by a man dressed in black.

Each coffin of a fallen one draped in our Union Jack,
Soldiers that played their part in Afghan's troubled land.

Our soldiers with courage did their very best to serve the Queen's flag.
Their lives cut short whilst serving in a foreign land.

As Bassett pays its tributes as bodies are brought by, sadness and grief
Soon slowly turns to anger as questions are asked WHY?
Why did someone's child? Why did they need to die?

Our politicians should take time and give the matter thought,
And think of all the misery to the loved ones they have brought.

Especially thought to a mother's tears who watched their child grow
     from birth to man
Shed their parting tears.
They send our lads to a battle in a war that we cannot win or end!

Is it time to end this war and bring our loved ones home
A war that is not of our making costs so many, many lives?

We need to ask for the reasons why?
Why they need to fight and die in a foreign land.
We hope and pray for our loved one's sake that the war will finally end,
With final prayer to the fallen who died in Afghan's troubled land.

We need to remember the brave fallen and to remember their brave names.
But for now hundreds of strangers will continue to stand at the street of
    Wootton Bassett
To greet and mourn for the brave fallen home with incredible respect.

We hope this war will finally end so no more mother's tears are shed.
We need to remember and never forget the brave fallen who died in Afghan's
    troubled land!

Let's wait a minute, let's pause a moment. Let us not forget!
Our other still serving soldiers still fighting in Afghan's troubled land.

Let us say a silent prayer.

'Please Lord bring our brave soldiers back to us, Please Lord keep them safe!'
Hope Lord hears our silent prayers and returns all our brave soldiers back home
    safe.

Age 13.

Oh Dear Sweet Child Of Mine

Oh dear sweet child of mine,
The first time I held this little new life of mine
And into these new little eyes I gaze and whisper how beautiful and perfect this little
  new life of mine.

Oh dear sweet child of mine,
As I watched and support the many years of your life
As I watch you grow and thrive and develop skills for your own life.

Oh dear sweet child of mine,
An adult now and now decide your own path of life
Oh how proud am I of this dear sweet child of mine.

Oh dear sweet child of mine,
As I say my tearful goodbyes as you go
And fight and support the Queen's troops in a foreign land
Oh dear God please keep safe and watch over my dear sweet child of mine.

Oh dear sweet child of mine,
My heart breaks as I stand and moan over your grave and say my final painful
  goodbyes
And ask a painful question why,
Why take my dear sweet child of mine?

Oh I love you my dear sweet child of mine!

Oh dear sweet mother of mine,
Don't grieve, don't dishearten, don't despair for me!
I now walk on the path of no pain, no fear I am by the light
Please don't cry don't lengthen your tears
Oh dear sweet mother of mine.

Think of me as not being far
I will always be in your memories your heart
I love you oh dear sweet mother of mine
We will see each other again but for now goodbye
Oh dear sweet mother of mine!

MICHAEL McKENZIE

Soul Mates

The soldier lay dying
With the padre by his side
He takes the soldiers hand
And says do not cry.

I am not sad father
Just so far from home
My love is not here
She must face this alone.

I will never again
Feel the soft of her kiss
The warmth of her heart
Or the love that she gives.

Trying to hold on, I am.
Till she reaches my side
I must say I love you
Just one last time.

To promise her, my love
That for all of time
I'll be her guardian angel
My soul mate, she's mine.

You brought me happiness, I say
You completed my life
Now that you are here
I am not afraid to die.

I love you I say
The flag of my life coming down
To rest at half mast
As the 21 guns sound.

Stay with me she pleads
But it's already too late
For now I'm an angel
Every soldier's fate.

In a dream to her I visit
As I take her hand
I tell her I love you
Always will, always have.

I kiss her lips tenderly
She slowly awakes
With a smile and a tear
She now knows her fate.

I wished her the happiness
The whole world can bring
Just never forget me
Always carry my ring.

Till one day we will meet
After she has grown old
To hold me again
Her life story told.

In heaven we again meet
In eternal embrace
We both say I love you
That's true love. Soul mates.

JAMES MILTON

A New Jerusalem

I vowed to thee my country all earthly things above
I donned a soldier's uniform and left the ones I love
I took another's country
I stole another's land
And fought there with my countrymen
Who died amidst the sand
And though we went there willingly
War's flame that burnt so bright
Consumed my love of country
And faded into night

Yet now I've left the colours
I see the foe at last
Not those of other nations
Nor enemies long past
Our evil lies within us
Those men who can't see wrong
Who for the love of power
Will sacrifice the strong
They've cast away our history
They've torn up all our laws
And thrown our nation's young men
Into endless petty wars

But now's the time of reckoning
And now the tide has turned
Our faith shall be rekindled
False idols will be burned
And from the pain of suffering
And from lost innocence
We'll resurrect our country
Regain our inner sense
We will build a new Jerusalem
In this green and pleasant land
And our work will stand as legacy
To the dead left in the sand.

This poem was one of the critical turning points in adjusting to being a civilian and coming to terms with our intervention in Iraq and how it could be a force for positive change within our country. If we did make mistakes, if brave men and women were placed in danger and lost their lives for a less than worthy cause, then the most positive thing we can do with that sacrifice is to use it as an example of courage and to correct those things in our own country which led to them first being sent here.

A Soldier's Lot

Son would you be willing
To take up the monarch's shilling,
A serving of her majesty the Queen?

To continue the tradition,
Through triumph and derision.
Go where your Pa and Grandpa both have been.

See your best friend die
Whilst he looks you in the eye,
To satisfy a politician's pride?

View the face of war
And all that's been before,
Yet know the real villains won't be tried?

Be the one-night darling
Of that harlot called the press
And then to be forgotten on the morrow,

With their articles of glory
And pay cheques, fat like rats
Fed upon the images of death and sorrow.

Follow in the footsteps
Of two centuries of men,
A banner that has flown for Britain's freedom,

Then hear of its demise
Because we must all downsize,
And heroes in this day who really needs 'em? Be so very blind
To the one you left behind,
For the needs of love are constant, harsh and cruel

And when you've done your duty
You no longer have your beauty
She's gone, left you behind to play the fool.

But, if my words won't hold you back
And you've set yourself the track
To serve your country well, without regret

Remember this

When the hunting dog is old
He is cast into the cold
I hope your master, unlike his, does not forget.

This is one of my first poems and was inspired, at least in spirit, by Rudyard Kipling's
Tommy in which he outlines the contradictory way in which soldiers are treated by the
society they serve. Whilst everyone pays lip-service to their courage, they are often ill
used, their traditions ignored and once used up in the service of their country, they find
themselves cast aside. I wanted people to think twice before doing any of these things.

A Soldier's Prayer

God give me a bird
And some booze and a bed
And a tv with Sky
In a house by the Med

And my mates in that same house
With birds and booze too
And a town down the road
Where there's something to do

Not this bunk in this camp
The sand and the waste
That gets in the air
Gives all food the same taste

Nor the heat and the wire
The grey sullen looks
As we tab down the streets
Past the shops and the souks

Or the threat of an ambush
Being bumped unaware
The car bombs and mortars
This slow grinding fear

For the bullet that gets you's
Not the one that you hear
And the blast from the bomb
Never reaches your ear

In fact God forget it
I see I've been greedy
In war as in life
It don't pay to be needy

Birds and booze come and go
That's a plain simple fact
Just get me home safely
My bollocks intact.

This is a soldier's prayer because we're soldiers, not saints. It's all about the basics.

Child's Play

Sing a song of Helmand
A death trap for the Brits

Car bombs on the corner
And food that gives you squits

The money for the lads' kits
Was squandered on MPs

So instead of helicopters
We have ornamental trees.

Because you can't believe what the MPs were spending their money on whilst 19 year-olds were being blown up in Afghanistan. It would be funny if it wasn't true.

Death Or Dishonour

We give no thought
When we're caught short
In London or in Rome
We just nip in
With a cheeky grin
To a shop or someone's home
But if nature calls
When you're under fire
And you reckon you're a gonner
You face the most
Unsavoury choice
Between death and dishonour.

A soldier, clearly suffering from dysentery shuffled out of the medical building and towards one of the latrines only five minutes after a mortar attack had finished. Upon reaching the latrine, he entered and there was a long and strangled yelp. The Sgt-Major sitting next to me lit up a cigarette and turned to me and said, 'Aye sir, there's another soul what's lost the battle between death and dishonour'. I thought it was a fantastic description of the choice.

Coming Home

There'll be no extra drill now,
No PT and no bull,
No stagging on in barracks
Or going on the pull.

No gripping from the Sergeant,
No scoff in the canteen.
You've done your final duty,
Your record's true and clean.

And the boys will gather round now
To see you on the plane,
Away from dirt and misery,
Away from dust and pain.

Your family will be waiting,
Your girl will wear her best,
As we take you back to hearth and home
To lay you to your rest.

This poem took me a year and a half to write. It was, if not inspired, then in memory of a young Private I never met, who died, aged 19 on an operation I was attached to, based out of Camp Dogwood with the Black Watch in November 2004. At the start of the operation, we were conducting vehicle checks as we had done in the South of Iraq when the order came through for us to pull back from the roads. A suicide bomber had driven into one of our checkpoints and detonated, killing three soldiers, an Iraqi interpreter and wounding half a dozen more in that action and a follow-up attack. The proximity of the operation to Christmas, the fact that the Black Watch thought they were going home and the age of the young soldier struck very deeply and I remember on R&R, leaving the cinema with my family, being overwhelmed by a feeling of loss for those whose loved ones never made it back. This poem is the result of that.

The Wife's Prayer

Teach me not to love you
I don't want to grieve
Please turn my heart to stone
Every time you have to leave

Packed upon a plane
Taken from my life
When you become a warrior
I would not be your wife

I would not sit awake at night
I could sleep sound instead
But your absence is too obvious
Alone in this empty bed

Every time I'm at a party
I'll remember you're not there
All those moments you would comfort me
Run fingers through my hair

The good times and the bad ones
When we'd shout at one another
I miss the things you mean to me
Husband, friend and lover

Kill off my flames of passion
Let each die out in turn
Then teach me how to love again
Upon your safe return.

This is a counter weight to the 'Soldier's Prayer', the unseen fears that all of the family have to deal with when their loved ones are on tour.

NEALE MOSS

A Time For Reflection

Years of hatred and fighting.
The Russians, Taleban, Mujahadeen and Americans,
The Brits, Canadians, French and Aussies,
The Romanians, Italians, Germans and Koreans,
The Japanese, Irish, Spanish and Dutch,
Even Greeks and Turks together,
Have all witnessed the terrible destruction
Of the once beautiful land,
In the lee of the Hindu Kush.

Houses reduced to rubble,
Roads to potholed tracks,
Farmland to dusty minefields,
Proud soldiers to crippled beggars,
Tanks to rusty bent skeletons.
All grotesque reminders of a long war,
In the once beautiful land in the lee of the Hindu Kush.

War that turned children into warriors,
Warlords into mighty barons,
The land into blowing dust.
The wind blew,
But no kites flew,
And the women hid beneath robes of blue,
In the once beautiful land of the Hindu Kush.

Now the kites are flying.
The houses are homes.
The roads are repaired.
The land is yielding crops.
The markets are full.
The children return to school,
In the beautiful land of the Hindu Kush.

What will next year bring?
Will the kites still fly high?
The children laugh and sing?
The women still hide?
Or, will the friendly Afghan,
In the beautiful land of the Hindu Kush,
Be forgotten – for Bin Laden and Bush?

LIAM O'BRIEN

The War In My Head

The war in my head seems unfair
Something I live with, but cannot share
Heartache and sadness I cannot cope
The tablets and therapy are filled with hope

At night the demons come to light
Trying to sleep, but still in the fight
Woken with sweats dreaded with fear
Faces pale, soaked with a tear

To me my life will never be the same
Always flooded with guilt, and dreaded shame
Watching people live, and having all their fun
It seems to hit me hard
Am I the only one?

The feeling I get when it comes to a head
Wouldn't it be better if I were just dead?
All I want is a better life
For me, my head, and my future wife.

PHOENIX

The Reality Of The Unreality...

They come at night the 'Ghosts' of comrades past of 'victims' to sit and stare at the end of the bed to ensure the shame guilt and regret continue – do they come on purpose, or are they conjured up by this broken mind as punishment for having lived for having killed?

They come in the day he sees them everywhere he hears them all the time and if they hide and remain silent they will send a smell just to remind him that they are there....in the shadows of his broken mind

The doctors say that they are following government guidelines with the medication that they give, they go through the motions of seeing him but nothing changes he remains in medicated zombie limbo a broken man a body complete with a mind in pieces

He wants to die he's found the place he'll dress in black so that the train driver will not see him, but does he really want to die or does he just want someone to listen to him to give him hope – take charge of him just like when he was in the Army?

He's become a victim of not only PTSD but the pride that the Army instils, ' You need no-one son apart from your Army Family, we look after you and you look after yourself and your comrades....what do civvies know?'

Told when to eat when to sleep no bills to pay no food to buy he's sent ill-equipped back to the land of the civvies.

Abandoned by the 'Family' misunderstood by civvies he finds himself on the streets, unkempt, unwashed with no direction spiralling down into a maelstrom of flashbacks panic attacks seeking solace in alcohol. He sleeps in doorways, on benches a once proud man now even more fractured by the shame of the man he has become...will this ever end can he bring it to an end?

He is a self-fulfilling prophecy – he is everything they say he should be because he has PTSD

The PTSD defines him, in the end he lets it, it is safer to stay like this than to try and move on, the fear is a monster much bigger than any courage he has ever had

The doctors in civvy street 'know nothing what can they do?' he cannot see that they will never learn if men like him will not let them, will not tell them what 'it' is like...he must teach them but he will not 'they are civvies what do they know?' and round in circles we go again.

The emotional rollercoaster he rides each day is exhausting, to survive another day is not seen as an achievement it is seen as a punishment, he will not forgive himself, he is unworthy of forgiveness.

To love a man like this means that you know when to keep quiet, you never ask questions, you are always aware that the man sitting by your side is not there, his body may be but his mind is back in Iraq, Bosnia, Northern Ireland....can you reach him bring him back, make a difference save his soul?

There are days when you want to say 'I can give no more, I do not know what I can do, I am this close to walking away'

But I can not, I will not abandon him....for he is worthy.

THOMAS ROBERTS

Bulletin

Reports of casualties have been confirmed
by authorities in Afghanistan.
The soldiers' next of kin have been informed.

An intense summer campaign is feared
from intelligence on Southern Helmand.
Reports of casualties have been confirmed.

I know one of their number, he was famed
at school for chess, all-in-all a quiet man.
The soldiers' next of kin have been informed.

I see him in stillness, his silhouette fired
before the fury of a red-raw sun.
Reports of casualties have been confirmed.

We were close, but our childhood friendship frayed,
its threads stretched beyond common boundary stones.
The soldiers' next of kin have been informed.

Writers evoked such loss with Troy in flames,
so is this what it means to be a human?
Reports of casualties have been confirmed.
The soldiers' next of kin have been informed.

MICHAEL RODGERSON

Weep For The Soldier

Weep for me now oh my proud lovely lady
Weep for me now for I'm gone far away
Over that dark hill and down where it's shady
Eternity's time, evermore and a day

Tell our dear children my love was unending
They will not know now the man that I've been
Sorrow is brief for them, mercy is lending
Cushioned forgetfulness of what they've seen

I will not be there to watch all their growing
No more soft moments and innocent eyes
Always it has to be you that they're knowing
On your slim shoulders their future relies

This is no place for young men to be dying
Barren and hopeless without any care
Seeing such waste all the world should be crying
Scoured of love this is hell and writ bare

So then weep for me now as the next day is dawning
Weep for a while and then please dry your tears
Think of me happily each bright new morning
Glad that we had those brief, wonderful years.

STEVE SELL

Cry For Me Not

Goodbye my love, cry for me not
for 'tis with pride I bear my lot,
'tis to lands afar that I must go,
 to distant lands, our flag to show.
'Tis for your freedom I leave this shore
to fight an enemy in a bloody war,
and to defend your liberty, I will be bold
and fight with honour, for the values we hold.
Peace with liberty which is our right,
it's for these values I'm proud to fight,
I know the struggle will be hard and long
and I pray the Lord will keep me strong.
And when again our flag is risen,
when the fighting is over
prayers will be given,
by those who have survived this dread
for those now, our glorious dead.
And for our enemies in those dark days
that they now see, the error of their ways,
for one day a world, where war is unknown
and where peace-loving men can remain at home.
But cry for me not, if I ne'er return
for my place in heaven, I shall have earned.

This Is My Field Now

It's quiet now,
but how long will it last?
The firing has stopped,
and so have the screams.
So still now, this cursed ground.
It's quiet now,
but how long will it last,
is the war over, finally, at last?
In the distance, a tearful moan,
another poor soul
so far from home?
It's quiet now,
but at what cost?
How many precious lives were lost?
What worth is an acre of cloying mud,
paid for with human blood?
It's quiet now,
and I make one wish,
before I go please grant me this:

Just a gentle kiss will suffice
as I ease painfully from this life,
a sweet caress, a word of calm,
my head resting on a feminine arm.
A kindly voice to sooth my fears
a gentle hand to brush my tears.
Bid me farewell, adieu, goodbye,
But please, don't leave me alone to die.

It's quiet now,
and time has gone by,
will anyone remember me,
after I die?

This is my field now,
my own domain,
and I need never,
to fight for it again.

KEVIN SMYTHERS

They Serve – For Our Freedom...

Terror lives on every street
yet harmony's in the home
outside the bombs and mortars blast
on avenues none dare roam

Into this maelstrom, men are sent
in truth, just boys with nerve
they know their lives are on the line
but they signed up to serve

With careful eyes, watching all
they set out on patrol
they see around them tree-lined streets
where people used to stroll

But now, each tree becomes a threat
a place for some to hide
the commanding base that sets the fire
or gives the mortars guide

Too many men and boys have served
and then failed to return
their lives submitted for ideals
that terrorists can't learn

Revere them, for they save us all
and pay a heavy price
to them it isn't 'Just a job'
so stop, and just think twice

Think once for all those brave young souls
at rest, remembered well
and think again for those left alone
wives and mothers who went through hell

Do not forget that sacrifice
that signifies their glory
they never sought fame, but justice
and that's their true life story

Give aid and succour without regard
for cost or complication
to those who find they're left behind
...it's the duty of the nation.

JANE STEMP

Waiting For The Truce

Star in the east
over the trenches shining
so far from Bethlehem
so far from home

Only the shells
over the trenches flying
the doves have faltered now
when will peace come?

Across the years
over the miles still yearning
from trench to sangar, all
hopes are the same

Bring us safe home
even from distant Helmand,
nearer to Bethlehem
still far from peace.

BARBARA STOCKER

Day Of Remembrance

I knelt down beside your grave
My head held high with pride
Once again we were together
Two brothers, side by side
I recalled the day I lost you
Memories so painful and raw
A flashback that still haunts me
Of the horrors that I saw
There, in your final moments
Of confusion, dust and heat
I could hear you cry out in pain
Then suddenly your heart ceased to beat
I feel so empty and lost
Without you, my brother, my best friend
Now you have gone forever
And my heart needs time to mend
And on this day of remembrance
I touch your name engraved in stone
Never to be forgotten –
Rest peacefully now, you're finally home.

MARK THURLEY

The Journey

Outward bound, on a journey from home,
From shelter and comfort, to chaos unknown
From all that is us, to those that need hope
Thoughts so now, thoughts boiling.

Outward bound, on a journey with an end?
In a place with others, in a cocoon of isolation
A mass of life on a flight to destiny
Thoughts so near, thoughts so far.

Outward bound, on a journey to discovery
Heavenly views of a world existing.
Life below happening, feeling unknowing.
Thoughts so deep, thoughts so demanding.

Outward bound, on a journey from love
Pages of words exploding, promising to return
Openness of feelings, regrets and desires
Thoughts so hard, thoughts denied.

Outward bound on a journey to an end.
Mortality so real, light so clean
Every moment a miracle, every known precious
Thoughts flowing, life living...

SHEILA WEBB

The Humble Poppy

Little poppy, ever red
Remind us of our glorious dead
For every bloom in each lapel
Heroic story you could tell.
Though seemingly a humble flower
Pay homage to 'our finest hour'.
Little poppy worn with pride
Heroes standing side by side
These mighty men we praise today
As silently in peace they lay. We hail these men we never knew God bless the many
    and 'the few'.
Little poppy through the land let heart and soul go hand in hand
As silently we stand in awe
Remembering those who went before
Released a while from heavenly host
Amid the strains of 'The Last Post'.

Two Minutes' Silence
We Must Remember Them

Two minutes' silence out of one day
A fair exchange each year we pay
In less than the time our egg to boil –
For a young man's death on foreign soil.
Two minutes' silence we put aside
To honour those who bravely died
In less than the time to toast a slice
We remember who paid the ultimate price.
Two minutes' silence and we all stand still
Some may not but others will
In less than the time to wait for a bus –
We thank the soldiers who died for us.
Two minutes' silence on November eleven
Our heroes we praise from Scotland to Devon
In less than the time these words to pen –
Then enjoy our lives – that we owe to them.

Stand And Be Counted

Beyond our horizon to stark Eastern sun
Set deep in the mountains, our story's begun
A hot burning desert, a desperate place
Where the Devil himself shows his face.

Axis of Evil where beauty is crushed
And flowers of the desert lay still in the dust
Brothers in arms brush the sand from their gun
With hearts beating loud as a drum.

Your wounds we will bathe and your scars we will heal
We'll carry you slowly, your pain we can feel
We'll call you a hero you'll reach for the sky
Way up to the stars you can fly.

Our soldiers returning, we're counting them all
In numbers on paper a valiant roll call
Loved ones and brothers and each mother's son
We're counting you home one by one.

Stand and be counted
and march side by side
The road paved with heroes
leads to the front line
Shoulder to shoulder a shield we will be –
Your flag and your country and me.

A shield of defiance that's made up of three –
YOUR FLAG, YOUR COUNTRY AND ME.

Wootton Bassett – A Salute

The grass here isn't greener
The streets not paved with gold
But lined with those in mourning
For the valiant and the bold.
A market town in Wiltshire brings
The country to its knee
As it marks each soldier's passing
In silent dignity.
A hush befalls the High Street
Bartholomew bids farewell
And casts his saintly shadow
Saluting those who fell.
The tenor bell tolls soulfully
It calls upon its folk
To remember fallen heroes
Draped in the union cloak.
Some stand tall in homage
Whilst others in silence lay –
The honourable and the honoured
We praise you both today.

War Memorial

Tread gently past the concrete names
   Chiselled amid the flowers
And take the time to ask yourself
   What were their final hours? Were they cradled by their loved ones –
      Holding a loving hand?
Or were they lying scared, alone
   Upon a foreign land?
Did they lie amidst the leaches
   Under a searing sun?
Or fall on a hostile mountainside
   In Iraq or Afghanistan? Today we praise the 'fallen'
      The many and the 'few'
The young, the brave, the valiant
   The ones we never knew. And every blood-red poppy
Worn in each lapel
Represents a **thousand** –
A thousand men who fell
But numbers are just numbers
It's the names we can't forget
As they are set in concrete
Like our everlasting debt.

SONJA WHALEN

A Sad, Silent Miracle

When you look at the sky
Do you pray?
Do you ask why?
I wonder what he'd say
If he ever answered
In a voice that would satisfy you
Down on your knees you fall
Waiting for some spectacle
Some proof of magic
Big bright lights
And jiggling bells
But miracles aren't noisy
They don't come with a spotlight
Sometimes they're dressed in tragedy
Sometimes they go unnoticed
God doesn't speak in words for a reason
He speaks with action, and in-action
Because those are much more powerful
And much more subtle
Thank him and be on your way
Later you may look back
And see this hardship
As what it really is
A silent, sad miracle.

My Dear Lost Picture

I run
But not away
I fight
And am here to stay
My enemy shall fall
Or I will die
My picture is lost
Only then do I cry
My days are numbered
But so are yours
My loved ones are safe
As long as the blood spilt is ours
Homesickness is my worst enemy
That picture was my only friend
In this lonely place
I can already see I'm about to bend
But my loneliness will subside
As soon as I see the whites of your eyes
And I watch them fade
As my homeland's threat slowly dies
All this to save my family from harm
I wish I could gaze on their faces once more
Before my end
My heart is sore
From the loss of my dear picture.

ROSA WILLIAMS

Friend's Soliloquy 1943

'Carpet rags needed for blind veterans'
That is what my paper said tonight.
And I sit here and ponder, I see
the battered forms yonder of America's beloved youngsters,
Black, brown and white,
stumbling along because they have no sight.

'Carpet rags needed for blind veterans.'
Dear God in Heaven!! Are wars never to end?
Is the 'Hill of Mars' to always be so rough and steep?
That their helping hands and gentle feet always be
bruised and spurned aside when they only want to go forward
to help a stricken friend.

'Carpet rags needed for blind veterans'
My heart is filled with pain and sorrow as I envision them.
Tomorrow, fumbling with those numerous rolls of strings
from which they will fashion many beautiful things.
I curse the cruel blindness which all wars bring.

'Carpet rags needed for blind veterans'.
Yes I am quite sure that's what my paper said.
I know it was meant to be a useful worth, but it should
have been a flamboyant announcement!
To seek this aid, it should have read:
'Let us give them the veils we borrowed from the Blue Fairy instead'.

The carpet rags this gentle Scottish mother was referring to, were the strips of cloth given to the veterans in the hospitals to use to make rag rugs.

Chosen by her granddaughter, Kelly Whittaker.

About the Authors

Sally Ainsworth

Sally wrote these poems from the heart, as at times she has found her son's first tour very difficult – just like thousands of military mums. She salutes our heroes fighting all over the world, but also the parents because while they are away fighting, they have to try to engage in normal family life, which can be very difficult.

Leading Seaman Mark Andrews (Royal Navy)

Mark joined the Royal Navy in 1990 as a Seaman Sonar. He wrote his poem while transiting the Suez Canal towards the Red Sea at the start of a six-month deployment in 2002 to the Arabian Gulf in support of Coalition operations concerning Iraq. They also indirectly supported operations in the Indian Ocean, with activity increasing in that area. His reason for writing the poem was simply to express how he felt that particular day. He recounts, '...everything slows down (in different ways) when transiting the Suez, so it is a time for reflection – mainly concerning our families and friends, whom we had said goodbye to not that long ago'.

Medical Assistant Mike Beavis (Royal Navy)

After the loss of a friend and fracturing his spine in an accident in the Falklands in 2005, Michael was left in hospital, several thousand miles from home. Suffering with survivor's guilt and being immensely frustrated with his situation, he started to write his feelings down – and they came out in rhymes.

Once back on his feet, he served in Afghanistan on Op Herrick 5 and in Iraq on Op Telic 10, attached to a front-line Army unit. This provided him with lots of inspiration for further poems. After being operational as a radio-operator, he transferred to the Naval Medical branch to become a medic attached to the Royal Marines and 3 Commando Brigade. Being the 'Doc' with the Marines he often had to help the lads with more than just physical wounds, and was often used as a sounding board, or someone to talk to. Writing poems has become a way of releasing pressure and allowing him to get his feelings out in the open.

Writing poems is often frowned upon in a somewhat macho environment, but with the ever-increasing number of British casualties and the mental issues that can follow from the high tempo of operations, Michael has found that writing can often provide a link between the feelings of service-people and civilian personnel. It has helped him and he will continue as long as he has something to write about.

Laurence Binyon

Robert Laurence Binyon (1869 – 1943) was an English poet, dramatist, and art scholar. His most famous work, *For the Fallen*, is well known not least from its use in Remembrance Sunday services.

Binyon studied at St Paul's School, then read Classics (*Honour Moderations*) at Trinity College, Oxford, where he won the Newdigate Prize for poetry in 1891.

Immediately after graduating in 1893, Binyon started working for the Department of Printed Books of the British Museum, writing catalogues for the museum and art monographs for himself. Many of Binyon's books produced while at the Museum were influenced by his own sensibilities as a poet, although some are works of plain scholarship.

For The Fallen was first published in The Times on September 21 1914. Laurence Binyon wrote it while working at the museum, and did not go to the Western Front until 1916, as a Red Cross orderly.

Neil Blower

Neil Blower is a British author, screenwriter and novelist, based in Manchester. He joined the British Army when he left school and served five years with the Royal Tank Regiment, serving on operations in Kosovo and the 2003 Invasion of Iraq. Neil is currently studying for a degree in English Literature and Creative Writing at the University of Salford – where he found out he was dyslexic.

His first novel, *Shell Shock: The Diary of Tommy Atkins,* was released in October 2011 by FireStep Press – an imprint of FireStep Publishing. He is now working on his second book, *My Subject is War,* which is a collection of short stories exploring the realities of contemporary conflict.

Julia Bond

Julia Bond has been married for 20 years and has three children. Her husband Jon is currently in Afghanistan. Julia has been involved with the Army all her life – her father was in the Army and she herself served in the Army for a short time before marrying her husband. She currently lives in Northern Ireland.

Peter Branson

Peter Branson's poetry has been published or accepted for publication by journals in Britain, USA, Canada, Eire, Australia and New Zealand, including *Acumen, Ambit, Envoi, Magma, The London Magazine, Iota, Frogmore Papers, The Interpreter's House, Poetry Nottingham, Pulsar, Red Ink, The Recusant, South, The New Writer, Crannog, Raintown Review, The Huston Poetry Review, Barnwood, The Able Muse and Other Poetry.*

His first collection, *The Accidental Tourist,* was published in May 2008. A second collection was published at the beginning of 2010 by Caparison Press, and more recently a third collection has been accepted for publication by Salmon Press. He has won prizes and been placed in a number of poetry competitions over recent years, including firsts in the Grace Dieu and the Envoi International.

Michael Brett

During the Civil War in the former Yugoslavia, Michael Brett worked in the Press Section of the Information Centre of Bosnia-Herzegovina in London, promoting US and NATO military intervention. He believed in the ideal of a multi-ethnic Bosnian state and that it would stop the widespread massacres of civilians that were taking place at the time.

Michael attended Adrian Henri's Arvon class in 1976. He won the Iolaire Poetry Prize in 1983 and is one of the 2010 Winners of the Sampad (South Asian Arts) International Writing Competition. Random House have included some of his poems in the Ebury Book *Heroes: 100 Poems from the New Generation of War Poets*, edited by Carol Ann Duffy among others, published in 2011.

Michael was born in Accra, Ghana in 1955 and educated in England at Cranbrook School and the University of Reading, where he read English. He has a background in financial journalism, working in the City of London for over ten years, and continued to write throughout that period. He is currently Head of English at a school in South London.

Murray (Charlie) Brown

Charlie described himself as 'just a number' – so this is a biography of number 24583099.

Charlie was born in Hitchin in 1964 and his daughter was born while he was serving in Germany. Charlie was honoured with the British Empire Medal while serving in the Gulf for services above and beyond the call of duty. Having joined the Army in 1980, he left being medically discharged in 1994 after being diagnosed 'no longer fit to serve', due to 'Gulf War Syndrome' after the 1st Gulf War 1990/1991.

Charlie built his own website *www.the-gulf-war.com* where all the information of the time spent in the Gulf can be found.

'Served in faith, forgotten in haste'.

Lieutenant Colonel Jonathan Brown 'JB' (Army – Royal Logistics Corps)

Currently serving overseas, Lieutenant Colonel Jonathan Brown MSc is a British Army Officer in the RLC.

In 24 years, 'JB' has served in numerous countries including the UK, Germany, Canada, USA, Oman, throughout Europe, Cyprus, the Falkland Islands, Afghanistan, Bosnia and Kosovo. Operationally, he has served in Northern Ireland on Op Banner twice, on Op Granby during the Gulf War, and Baghdad in 2008-09. He was the Commanding Officer of 7 Regiment RLC in Germany and during this time he deployed as CO, Sector 2, UNFICYP in Cyprus.

'JB' started writing poetry in his teens. He has two previously published poems and was a featured poet in the *Sunday Times Magazine* in November 2008. He is soon to publish a collection through FireStep Publishing.

Katie Butler-Manuel

Wilfred Owen's poem *Dulce et Decorum est* really moved Katie when she was studying war poems in English at school, so she decided to write a poem about the horrors of war. She lives in the East Sussex village of Catsfield with her parents, grandfather and two older brothers. She wrote *War* as a twelve-year-old pupil at St Andrew's school in Eastbourne. She has always enjoyed reading and writing poetry and is thrilled that her poem has been selected to appear in this anthology in aid of such a fantastic cause.

Daniel Clayton

Daniel Clayton was born in the summer of 1992. He comes from a military background, predominantly the Royal Engineers. Daniel has grown up in locations all over the world due to many overseas postings such as Cyprus, Belgium, Germany and the UK. He has recently completed his application for the British Army and is due to start his career in the British Army in October 2011.

Martin Crowson

Martin was born at a military hospital in Singapore in 1957, where his father was serving in the Royal Signals. He served himself for seven years, joining the Royal Army Medical Corps in 1970, going to Ireland in 1975 until March 1976 and to Germany when he returned.

He wrote the poem with a mixture of sentiment for his father's time at war during the 1940's and his own taste of conflict – albeit civil unrest in Northern Ireland. His father Raymond received a gunshot wound to his leg during the fighting against the Japanese, and following this served his time in a Japanese POW Camp. Martin did not get shot or wounded, but some of his close friends did, one very good friend losing his life in service and Martin draws on these experiences to write his poetry.

He wrote *A Soldier's Battle Thought* after having thoughts on his own active service in Northern Ireland. Although it does not depict the war in Northern Ireland, it is inspired by the Second World War and his father's experience of being wounded and imprisoned.

Jo De Vries

Jo wrote this poem in 2010, inspired by a close friend who was serving in the Intel Corps in Kabul at the time, and who sent her an email on Valentine's Day.

She has worked in military history publishing for nearly 10 years and has recently completed an undergraduate Diploma in Literature and Creative Writing through the Open University. In her spare time she also enjoys rifle target shooting and raising money for Help for Heroes on behalf of a number of friends and colleagues serving in the Armed Forces. Jo is married and lives in Gloucestershire.

George Douglas

A Mother's Soldier Comes Home came about while George was watching the all-too-familiar sight of the sad procession through Wootton Bassett. At the end of the news article they zoomed in on a red rose lying in a rain puddle – a sight he could not forget. Sadly, George passed away in 2011 before this anthology was published.

Corporal Steven Firkins (Army – 101 Engineer Regiment, Explosive Ordnance Disposal)

Corporal Steven Firkins joined the Army in 1995 and served in Northern Ireland, Iraq in the second war and two tours of Afghanistan, where he is due to go return in 2012.

Ian Foulkes (AKA BlackDog661)

Ian joined the Royal Corps of Signals in 1980 and was trained at the Army Apprentices College Harrogate, graduating in 1982. He served mainly overseas, Germany, Northern Ireland and Norway being a few of his postings. He was also awarded a Commander-in-Chief's Commendation. Ian had many interesting and diverse roles both within Royal Signals and while detached. His final postings were UK-based and Ian finished his Army career in 1999, having reached the rank of sergeant.

Cleveland W. Gibson

Cleveland is a dedicated carer who enjoys writing in many genres and who has won awards for fiction. In January this year he won a poetry award from www.celj.org. Now Trestle Press are publishing his work as Digital Shorts. There is an audio tape too. Currently he is working on a Young Adult novel – *House of the Skull Drum*.

Ivor Gurney

Ivor Gurney, the son of a tailor, was born in Gloucester on 28 August, 1890. Gurney was educated at King's School, Gloucester as a chorister and won an open scholarship to the Royal College of Music in 1911. He showed considerable talent as a composer and poet.

On the outbreak of the First World War, Gurney volunteered for the Gloucester Regiment, but was initially turned down because of his defective eyesight. However, as the British Army was short of men, he was allowed to join in 1915. On 7 April 1917, Gurney was shot and sent to the Army hospital at Rouen. In July 1917 Gurney was transferred to the 184 Machine Gun Company and joined the Forces preparing for the offensive at Passchendaele. Gurney was gassed at St Julien on 10 September 1917. He was sent to Edinburgh War Hospital and while recovering wrote a collection of war poems, *Severn and Somme*, which appeared in November 1917.

After the war, Gurney spent time in the Newcastle General Hospital, Lord Derby's War Hospital in Warrington and the Middlesex War Hospital in St Albans. Gurney was finally discharged from hospital and the Army on 4 October 1918.

Gurney's second book of poems, *War's Embers* was published in May 1919.

Steve Halliwell

Steve Halliwell was born and bred in the city of Salford, Greater Manchester in 1952 and educated in one of the city's finest secondary schools. He served twelve years in the Grenadier Guards/RAOC, leaving in 1983. By 1986 Steve started losing his eyesight, finally being registered blind in 2007. His eldest son also served in the 2RRF. In 2009 2RRF lost seven men in Afghanistan, and the mother of one of the fallen (Sergeant Simon Valentine) asked if Steve could help with fundraising – which rekindled his interest in writing.

Jodie Henderson

Jodie has been interested in photography for a couple of years, especially wildlife subjects. Her interest started when she was a finalist in the RSPCA's Young Photographer of the Year competition in 2009. She wanted to pursue photography as a career, so when it came to her work experience week, she decided to try and get something related to photography. She was very grateful that she was offered a placement by Swindon Link magazine and professional photographer Richard Wintle of Calyx TV. Halfway through the week, she was assigned to photograph the repatriation ceremony of Highlander Scott McLaren of the 4th Battalion, the Royal Regiment of Scotland, who was killed in Afghanistan on 4 July 2011. Jodie had never been to a repatriation ceremony and was unsure what to expect. She found the day very emotional and wrote her poem to try to sum up how she felt, and what it was like for a fifteen-year-old to witness a repatriation. She will never forget standing on the roadside that day in Wootton Bassett, reflecting on the ultimate sacrifice made by so many servicemen and women.

Steven Leslie Hill

Steven Hill, a former operations construction manager, qualified as a horticulturist at Brackenhurst College, and is now self-employed as a landscape designer and horticulturist. He has had a lifelong interest in military history, particularly WW1, Vietnam, Ireland and the Holocaust. This, combined with his love of reading and poetry, inspired him to write *Foot Patrol* for the Paras, through a family contact who corresponds with 3 Para.

Steve regularly writes a feature on his other passion, wildlife conservation, for a local magazine in his area and his book of poetry, *Poems of World War One 1914-1918* is now on general sale.

Colonel TJ Hodgetts CBE MMEd MBA FRCP FRCSEd FCEM (L/RAMC)

Tim Hodgetts is an emergency physician with over 20 years of military operational experience in treating the victims of conflict in Northern Ireland, Kosovo, Iraq and Afghanistan. He has published and lectured extensively in the fields of pre-hospital care, disaster medicine, and resuscitation of the critically injured. His academic career includes the positions of inaugural Defence Professor of Emergency Medicine at the College of Emergency Medicine, Honorary Professor of Emergency Medicine at the University of Birmingham, and Penman Professor of Surgery at the University of Cape Town.

In 1999 he was made Officer of the Order of St John for services to humanity; in 2006 he was the national 'Hospital Doctor of the Year'; in 2009 he was made Commander of the British Empire for his contribution to combat casualty care; and in 2010 he received the Danish Defence Medal for Meritorious Service.

Tim's poems, written on serial deployments to Afghanistan and Iraq since 2002, reflect the physical, ethical and emotional challenges that face medical staff when working in the conflict environment, and when dealing daily with the human consequences of conflict.

Sergeant Dean Horton (Army – 16 Medical Regiment)

Dean Horton joined the Army in 2003 as a Combat Medical Technician (CMT) in the Royal Army Medical Corps (RAMC). During Dean's three years at 1 Close Support Medical Regiment, he passed All Arms Pre Parachute Selection (P Coy) and also deployed to Bosnia in 2005 and Afghanistan (Operation Herrick 4) in 2006.

While at 2 Para, Dean completed his jumps course and was awarded his British Jump Wings. He was also deployed to Afghanistan on Operation Herrick 8 with B Company and posted to 16 Medical Regiment and deployed on Operation Herrick 13 in Afghanistan, working with the Brigade Advisory Group. This job involved working in partnership with the Afghanistan National Army (ANA). Dean was attached to the Recce Platoon 1st Battalion Irish Guards, assisting the ANA Recce Platoon. On returning to the UK after Op Herrick 13 he was posted to OPTAG in Folkestone Kent where he currently serves as an instructor.

Dean wrote *The Airborne Medic's Creed* for many reasons. He has always been a front-line patrol medic on operations, and in doing this job has had the privilege of serving with some of the finest soldiers in existence. He has also had to treat some of these men – some of whom did not survive.

He wrote the poem while on Operation Herrick 13 and it is as a tribute to these men as well as his colleagues. He believes that any man who is willing to put his life on the line for his country deserves to have a medic equally as tenacious as he, ready to do battle with the Angel of Death should the worst happen. Dean has always believed this and it is what makes him strive to be the best medic he can be. He takes great pride in the Medics at 16 Medical Regiment, as they all maintain this attitude of striving to be the best, what they call the 'Airborne Attitude', and have time and time again done battle with – and defeated – the Angel of Death!

AE Housman

Alfred Edward Housman (1859 –1936), usually known as AE Housman, was an English classical scholar and poet, best known to the general public for his cycle of poems *A Shropshire Lad*. Lyrical and almost epigrammatic in form, the poems were mostly written before 1900. Their wistful evocation of doomed youth in the English countryside, in spare language and distinctive imagery, appealed strongly to late Victorian and Edwardian taste, and to many early twentieth-century English composers (beginning with Arthur Somervell) both before and after the First World War. Through its song-setting, the poetry became closely associated with that era, and with Shropshire itself.

Housman was counted one of the foremost classicists of his age, and has been ranked as one of the greatest scholars of all time. He established his reputation publishing as a private scholar and, on the strength and quality of his work, was appointed Professor of Latin at University College London and later at Cambridge. His editions of Juvenal, Manilius and Lucan are still considered authoritative.

Regimental Sergeant-Major Ian Jolley (Army – The Queen's Royal Hussars)
Staff Sergeant-Major Michael Malin (Army – The Queen's Royal Hussars)

In 2005 and not long after A Squadrons returned from peace-keeping duties in Cyprus, where Ian and Michael were deployed, the warrant officers and Sergeant's Mess held a ladies' dinner night. The Regiment had been told that, in early 2006 it was to deploy to Iraq on Op Telic 8, and as a part of the ladies' night Ian was tasked to write a poem.

Mikey Malin is a very true and loyal friend to Ian (like a brother); no matter where he is, Mikey has always been there. In 2006 Ian's call-sign was involved in an IED blast in Basrah and Mikey's call-sign was there supporting them within minutes, putting his own call-sign in harm's way in order that they could hold the ground, administer casualties and extract them safely. Mikey and Ian arrived at the poem you now have, with Ian delivering it to the Mess on the ladies' dinner night, where it was received very well. Due to the way in which it was received and being asked for copies, they decided to distribute it among the families in the Regiment, again this was received well and Ian has attempted to promote it more widely since.

Rudyard Kipling

Rudyard Kipling (1865-1936) was born in Bombay, but educated in England at the United Services College, Westward Ho, Bideford. In 1882 he returned to India, where he worked for Anglo-Indian newspapers. His literary career began with *Departmental Ditties* (1886), but subsequently he became chiefly known as a writer of short stories. A prolific writer, he achieved fame quickly. Kipling was the poet of the British Empire and its yeoman, the common soldier, whom he glorified in many of his works, in particular *Plain Tales from the Hills* (1888) and *Soldiers Three* (1888) – collections of short stories with roughly and affectionately drawn soldier portraits. His *Barrack Room Ballads* (1892) were written for, as much as about, the common soldier. In 1894 appeared his *Jungle Book*, which became a children's classic all over the world. *Kim* (1901), the story of Kimball O'Hara and his adventures in the Himalayas, is perhaps his most felicitous work. Other works include *The Second Jungle Book* (1895), *The Seven Seas* (1896), *Captains Courageous* (1897), *The Day's Work* (1898), *Stalky and Co.* (1899), *Just So Stories* (1902), *Traffics and Discoveries* (1904), *Puck of Pook's Hill* (1906), *Actions and Reactions* (1909), *Debits and Credits* (1926), *Thy Servant a Dog* (1930), and *Limits and Renewals* (1932).

During the First World War Kipling wrote some propaganda books. His collected poems appeared in 1933. Kipling was the recipient of many honorary degrees and other awards and in 1926 received the Gold Medal of the Royal Society of Literature, which only Scott, Meredith, and Hardy had been awarded before him.

JG Magee

Anyone who has ever flown an airplane is likely to be familiar with and value the poem *High Flight*, which was written in 1941 by Pilot Officer John Gillespie Magee, Jr. The reason for this sonnet's durable popularity among pilots is that it has been found by many to give unique and felicitous expression to the emotions aroused by the act of piloting an aircraft.

Although this poem was inspired by the experience of flying a Spitfire over England during the period following the Battle of Britain, it has since become familiar to pilots everywhere, many of whom regard it as a kind of prayer.

In 1940, John elected to join the RCAF as an American volunteer and spent most of the following year training in Canada. After obtaining his wings in mid 1941, he was transferred to South Wales, via the Personnel Reception Centre at Bournemouth, for some final training. Shortly afterwards he was assigned to active service in the newly formed Number 412 RCAF Fighter Squadron, based at Digby, Lincolnshire.

While John was stationed at Digby, he was asked to test-fly a newer model of the Spitfire V, which was capable of flying at an altitude of 30,000 feet. This experience evidently made such an impression on him that it provided the inspiration for his final poem, and best-known work, the sonnet *High Flight*.

John was killed in a mid-air collision during practice manoeuvres on 13 December 1941, just six days after the United States entered the war.

The poem was displayed in early 1942 in an exhibition of poetry at the Library entitled 'Faith and Freedom'. The manuscript copy of *High Flight* remains at the Library of Congress and *High Flight* has since appeared in many anthologies and books of quotations.

Paul Marlow

Having served in the military, making two tours in Bosnia, Paul's life was in disarray at the sights and experiences of combat. On leaving the Forces, he roamed wildly across the world, losing himself in his own turmoil, delving deep into the madness of alcoholic bliss and running from everything he knew and loved until the breaking point, where he chose to live!

Now having gone through a recovery programme and settling into some sort of normalcy, both through his addiction and post traumatic stress disorder, Paul has found a friend in writing about his decisions in combat and the day-to-day life of living with the choices he has made.

Paul has just completed a BA Hons Degree in Creative Writing and is about to undertake the Masters in the same discipline. Through his poetry he hopes to give the reader an insight of what it is to be him, on a journey through his eyes.

Nigel Marshall

Sleeping out at Christmas is as much about Nigel as it is about any other soldier who comes back from a war-zone changed from what they used to be. Nigel was lucky – he never ended up on the streets – but that is where his path diverges from that of the 'begging drunk' in the poem. The rest of him is Nigel.

Since the age of five, Nigel aimed to join the Army, becoming the latest in a long line of soldiers from his family. He realised the ambition aged sixteen when he was accepted into one of the Army Apprentice Colleges. Nigel served seven years in the Army including the Gulf War in 1991. Unwilling to burden those around him by talking about what he had experienced, he took to writing poetry as a means of self-examination and of getting those experiences and feelings out.

He is a separated father of four children, although his first son died due to premature birth. He is currently employed as a coachbuilder in Leeds. He is also currently studying for a degree in History with the Open University, although his passion lies in the battlefields of the First World War, especially the area around the Belgian city of Ieper (Ypres), which fascinates him. Nigel's hobbies take him back to the battlefields regularly as he researches the role of the West Yorkshire Regiment in the war and the lives and experiences of the men from his village who are named on the local war memorials.

Paige McAlwane

Paige wrote these poems when she was thirteen years old. The inspiration behind the poems was the heartfelt news footage of seven British soldiers, killed in Afghanistan, being repatriated through Wootton Bassett. It was extremely moving to watch hundreds of people come to paid their respects. However, it wasn't just the story from Wootton Bassett that inspired her, but also her father because, without the help of Combat Stress he would not have received the help he needed.

Her father served nine years in the Army with the Royal Pioneer Corps. During that time he served three consecutive tours in Northern Ireland and served one tour in the First Gulf War and was injured during this time. They repaired the physical injuries but left the mental injuries untreated.

It was ten years before Paige's father sought help and finally had the courage to contact Combat Stress. They diagnosed her father with Post Traumatic Stress Disorder

(PTSD) but it had already made an emotional impact on her family's lives. Combat Stress played a huge role in helping her father and continues to support and help him to this very day.

They say time is the greatest healer, but it is helped along more so with a kind and patient ear and with the overwhelming support from Combat Stress and the Royal British Legion. Their helping hand was an added inspiration behind these poems. Paige hopes that Combat Stress will help others in the same situation. It takes courage to ask for help, but it is the first step to enable the healing to start. Her mother always says to her '...tomorrow is a new day, start your life as a new day! Hope is there, help is there, you only need to look and ask.'

Bombardier Michael McKenzie (Army – Royal Artillery)
Michael McKenzie is 26 years old and serves as a bombardier in the Royal Artillery, where he has been since 2002. He completed a tour of Iraq in 2003 and has travelled all over the world. He is currently an instructor at a phase-two training unit and hails originally from Ipswich.

James Milton
Captain Milton served eight and a half years as an officer in the British Army between 1998 and 2007, first in the Adjutant Generals Corps and then the Intelligence Corps. Between 2003 and 2006 he carried out three separate tours of Iraq, first as an Arabic Interpreter attached to a number of units, including the Black Watch during their month-long deployment in the blockade of Fellouja (November 2004), and subsequently as an Intelligence Officer. In 2005, he received the Joint Commander's Commendation in recognition for his efforts during his second tour of Iraq as Second in Command of the Interpreter's section of Multi-National Division South East. He now works for Rolls Royce.

Colonel Neale Moss OBE MBA BSc (Hons) CMgr FCMI (Army Air Corps)
Colonel Moss was the lead officer for the training of the Afghan National Army as part of a small team called the Afghan National Army Reconstruction Team (ANART) based first in Bagram and then in Kabul. This was during the latter half of 2002 and he wrote this poem during Ramadan because they could not work with the Afghans that day.

A third-generation Army pilot, Neale Moss was educated at Rossall School and RMA Sandhurst, before being commissioned into the Royal Artillery in 1976. After various tours, Neale volunteered for flying training and passed the course at Middle Wallop in 1984. Amongst his varied postings, Neale has been with 3 Regiment Army Air Corps based in Soest, Germany as a flight commander, then Adjutant, during which time he participated in Op Banner (NI) as City Flight Commander.

After a brief interlude in the UK as one of the authors of the Future of Air Manoeuvre Study, Neale was assigned to the Falkland Islands where he was responsible for updating plans and running exercises. He took command of Wattisham Station and the Attack Helicopter Force in April 2010 and is due to stay in Suffolk until April 2012.

He is responsible for raising funds for the Afghan Appeal Fund (AAF), which builds schools in Afghanistan and has been doing so since 2006. He has just (August 2011) finished cycling from Land's End to John O'Groats with his fifteen-year-old son, raising over £5,000 and increasing awareness for AAF. They cycled the 900 miles in just thirteen days. As well as being a Chartered Manager (CMI) he is an Upper Liveryman of the Guild of Air Pilots and Navigators (GAPAN).

Liam O'Brien

Born and raised in a small town in West Yorkshire, Liam left home at sixteen to join the RAF and went on to serve ten years as a chef doing tours in Kosovo, Afghanistan and Iraq, to name a few. Now he has left the military and is being treated by Combat Stress for PTSD due to the severity of the things he witnessed during his time in operational theatre. He has written this poem as it describes the way he had to deal with his everyday life, and he knows this will be the same for many other sufferers.

Phoenix

Phoenix is a woman who has been judged in the past for her actions but who chooses not to judge those whose actions were those of necessity. She loved and continues to love a man who thinks he is unworthy because the Mistress PTSD tells him so...

Thomas Roberts

Thomas Roberts is a poet living in London. He was born and brought up in Belfast.

Mike Rodgerson

Mike Rodgerson was born and still lives in the gorgeous Derbyshire Peak District and has two sons, a daughter and two grandsons.

Mike served from 1960 to 1965 as a ground radar fitter in the Royal Air Force and served in the UK and Germany. He is also a member of the Royal British Legion.

After working in electronics for many years he spent the last eight years of his working life as a management consultant until retiring in 2006. Mike started to write poetry about ten years ago and finds military themes very inspirational, but writes about many subjects as the mood takes him.

Siegfried Sassoon

Siegfried Loraine Sassoon CBE MC (1886 –1967) was an English poet, author and soldier. Decorated for bravery on the Western Front, he became one of the leading poets of the First World War. His poetry both described the horrors of the trenches, and satirised the patriotic pretensions of those who, in Sassoon's view, were responsible for a pointless war. He later won acclaim for his prose work, notably his three-volume fictionalised autobiography, collectively known as the *Sherston Trilogy*.

Steve Sell
Steve Sell is ex-Forces and ex-Police. He has been married for 38 years and has three children, two in the Police and one in the Army. Family is very important to him. Steve has had two or three pieces published in different anthologies and finds writing the perfect way to relax.

Kevin Smythers
Kevin Smythers served in the RAF from 1970 to 1976. On return to 'civvy street' he worked for many years as an electronics engineer in various industries, and is currently working in air-conditioning.

An occasional 'hobbyist' poet, writer and musician he says 'he has never dedicated himself to any one thing long enough to become any good at it'. His interest in the Forces has never waned, despite a long separation from that life. Through family and friends he has always retained some contact with the Forces and feels keenly for those who serve and endure.

Jane Stemp
Jane Stemp is a published novelist and short story writer who, under her married name, curates the Historic Collections Library of the Institute of Naval Medicine. In her spare time she reads, listens to music of all sorts and occasionally sails with the Jubilee Sailing Trust. She has a long-term interest in the Great War, but this poem was sparked by the death of a TA colleague in Afghanistan not long before Remembrance Day 2010 – another sad reminder that 'the war to end war' did no such thing.

Barbara Stocker
Barbara Stocker was born in Manchester. She had a typical military childhood with postings in the UK and Germany. Her father proudly served in the 14th/20th King's Hussars Regiment and later served with the Duke of Lancaster's Own Yeomanry.
Barbara was a Bank Official for over 21 years while living in Lancashire and Merseyside, but now currently lives and works in Barnstaple, North Devon.
Her love of poetry began from an early age, inspired by her beloved father. This is her first poem to have been published and she is sure her father would have been so proud of her.

Major Mark Thurley (Army – Royal Artillery)
The poem was written after the Iraq war in a writers' group. The group were challenged to write a poem, and this is Mark's first piece of writing about the experience of leaving a lovely family to go to a very dangerous location – and potentially not return.

Major Thurley left his family just after Christmas 2003 and spent New Year 2004 in Baghdad/Camp Babylon.

Sheila Webb

Sheila's daughter Sarah-Jane was an officer in the RAF before injuring herself at Cranwell. Although she 'passed out' and went on to Strike Command and RAF Halton she unfortunately had to be invalided out due to a recurring back injury from Cranwell.

Sheila's first RAF poem was sent to RAF Lyneham after a Hercules plane went down over Iraq, killing all officers on board. She was so moved by this that she had to put her feelings down. The Padre there phoned her and asked for it to be included in the memorial service. She was delighted and very moved. Since then Sheila has written many poems about our Forces and has even written and recorded a song, entitled *Stand and Be Counted*, in their honour. She has a poem at RAF Uxbridge about The Battle of Britain and also one at RAF Conningsby for the Red Arrows. Sheila has great empathy with our brave men and women, and loves expressing it in verse. Her local British Legion burnt down recently and she had a poem for them printed in the local paper. She has also had poems published in *The Daily Mail* and many have been about our Forces from which she has received support from the public. She works at a school and also for the elderly with Social Services so she is always very busy. Her love is for the written word, especially when it praises our Forces.

Sonja Whalen

Sonja Whalen is the youngest of eight children, and the proud daughter of a deceased Navy veteran. She is also the daughter of an author, and has always wished to follow in her mother's footsteps and become one herself. She is a proud member of the United States, born in California, and raised in the Missouri Ozarks.

Rosa Williams

Rosa Jane Williams, born in 1895 in Webster County, was the grandmother of Kelly Whittaker. In 1918, she and Kelly's grandfather went by covered wagon from West Virginia to the Panhandle of Oklahoma. They had ten children, seven boys and three girls. Out of the seven boys, five served in the Military.

One of Kelly's uncles, Burton, served in the Royal Air Force as a radio operator and was killed in WWII in the South of England. Rosa wrote for the area newspaper for over forty years and was known by the *Round About News*. She sadly went blind in her fifties but continued to write with the help of an assistant. Rosa passed away in 1967.

The Sentinels

'The little crosses on the hillside mark the rest billets of our comrades of the trenches. They haven't really left us; they are only on ahead, like scouts, finding the way. One day we will join them, and then they will guide us over "No Man's Land" into that friendly country of peace, rest and happiness. Meanwhile, they stand on guard along the battle front. Let us not forget.'

Lt-Col T. A. Lowe, DSO, MC, The Western Battlefields: A Guide to the British Line (London: Gale & Polder, 1920)

FIRESTEP
Publishing

FireStep Publishing is a new division of *Tommies Guides
Military Booksellers and Publishers*, first established in 2005
by Ryan Gearing. Our aim is to publish up to 100 books
and related product a year and bring new and old titles
alive for the military enthusiast whilst having the ability
and desire through many of our book projects to work
with and to suport HM Forces and related charities.

We offer an unparalleled range of services from
traditional publishing through to subsidised self-
publishing and bespoke packages for the discerning
and specialist author, historian, genealogist, museum or
organisation. We are always looking for new ideas and
ventures and especially welcome enquiries from military
museums and organisations with a view to partnering in
publishing projects.

We pride ourselves on our commitment to each book
and our authors, our professionalism and being able
to work solely within the military genre, with the
knowledge, contacts and expertise to maximise the
potential of any of our products.

**For more information on any of our titles,
to contact us with suggestions for new books,
or just to keep in touch please visit our website:
www.firesteppublishing.com**